Strouden Library

⌐ Hapoint

⌐ West

07/08

D0242061

ES

Friday's Child

Friday's Child

The Heartbreaking Story of a Mother's Love and a Family's Loss

Ben Palmer

Bournemouth Libraries

ST	
300011070	
Askews	2008
362.1987	£12.99

Published by Virgin Books 2008

2 4 6 8 10 9 7 5 3 1

Copyright © Ben Palmer 2008

Ben Palmer has asserted his right under the Copyright, Designs
and Patents Act 1988 to be identified as the author of this work

This book is a work of non-fiction based on the life, experiences and recollections of the author. In
some limited cases names of people have been changed solely to protect the privacy of others. The
author has stated to the publishers that, except in such minor respects not affecting the substantial
accuracy of the work, the contents of this book are true.

'Dancing Queen' lyrics reprinted by permission Bocu Music Ltd, 1 Wyndham Yard.
Composed by Anderson/Ulvaeus

The publisher has made serious efforts to trace the copyright owners of all material reproduced
in this book. Should any have inadvertently been overlooked the publisher would be happy to
acknowledge any rightful owner and would be grateful for any information as to their identity.

This book is sold subject to the condition that it shall not,
by way of trade or otherwise, be lent, resold, hired out,
or otherwise circulated without the publisher's prior
consent in any form of binding or cover other than that
in which it is published and without a similar condition,
including this condition, being imposed
on the subsequent purchaser.

First published in Great Britain in 2008 by
Virgin Books
Random House
Thames Wharf Studios,
Rainville Road
London, W6 9HA

www.rbooks.co.uk

Addresses for companies within The Random House Group Limited can be found at:
www.randomhouse.co.uk/offices.htm

The Random House Group Limited Reg. No. 954009

A CIP catalogue record for this book
is available from the British Library

ISBN 9781905264285

The Random House Group Limited supports The Forest Stewardship Council [FSC],
the leading international forest certification organisation. All our titles that are printed
on Greenpeace approved FSC certified paper carry the FSC logo. Our paper procurement
policy can be found at www.rbooks.co.uk/environment

Mixed Sources
Product group from well-managed
forests and other controlled sources
www.fsc.org Cert no. TT-COC-2139
© 1996 Forest Stewardship Council

Typeset by Palimpsest Book Production Limited,
Grangemouth, Stirlingshire

Printed and bound in the UK by CPI Mackays, Chatham ME5 8TD

For Harry and Emily.
Mummy in Heaven loves you both;
Friday's child is loving and giving.

> Here a phoenix lieth, whose death
> To another phoenix gave breath:
> It is to be lamented much,
> The world at once ne'er knew two such.

Composed for Jane Seymour, who died two weeks after the birth of Edward VI, most likely from childbed fever.

Contents

Introduction

I'm 34, healthy, a homeowner, intelligent and easy enough on the eye, apparently. I have two beautiful, well-behaved and healthy young children who laugh and bring joy to everyone they know. But I'm miserable. What the hell is the problem?

I'm a single parent, a widower. The cruellest label. And this is our new life and it just isn't fair: we didn't want or deserve it; we were so happy in our old one.

I'm writing this because it's cathartic. I'm writing it so that I don't ever forget the raw pain, which I know will subside given enough time. And so that Harry and Emily can learn, one day, what happened to make our life the way it is and why I am the way I am. I may never be able to say why, but at least I can tell them how. I hope life will get better for them. And for me.

I met Jessica – although I, like many of her friends, called her Percy or Perc (with a soft 'c') – among mutual friends in a Fulham pub on 12 February 1993, when we were both 22. I proposed, on bended knee with a diamond ring and roses, six years later, almost to the day.

We were married a little over five months later on a very hot day in late July and honeymooned in the Loire Valley and Ile de Ré, travelling about in Jessica's beloved 1974 MGB GT. We loved each other exclusively for nearly eleven and a half years in total – for richer, for poorer; in sickness and in health; till death us do part.

Cruelly, it did.

Anyone who has lost their soulmate or is a single parent will know that life can be a lot harder than I have had the ability to portray – I hope you will forgive the understatement.

Percy always wanted to write a book – 'Everyone has at least one book in them and one day I'll write mine,' she'd say. I know that hers would have been a period romance, but I hope that she would have been proud of my efforts.

From: Charles Palmer
To: Ben Palmer
Date: 22 June 2004 16:33
Subject: Good Luck

Hello Ben and Percy and Harry
Just to let you know that all West London is
looking forward to imminent newbie, and hop-
ing all goes well!
Much love,
Charlie xxx

From: Ben Palmer
To: Charles Palmer
Date: 22 June 2004 16:37
Subject: Re: Good Luck

Thank you! Little blighter's a day late -
bound to be a girl!
Love,
Ben

Dear Charlie,
I saw lots of policemens at school today.
Lots of love from,
Harry

Day 1:
Thursday, 24 June 2004

At 6.26 p.m. Jessica gave birth after a short and uncomplicated delivery and our world was made. The midwife held up 9lb 13oz of baby with dark, matted hair and a roll of fat around its neck, for Jessica to see.

'It's a boy!' she exclaimed. The midwife and I looked at each other in surprise.

'Look again, Jessica,' the midwife said.

'It's a girl! It's a girl!' Jessica laughed. She had so desperately wanted a daughter. It meant so much to her that she had given me a son three years earlier, and she now wanted a baby girl. Both of us would always have been happy with whatever children we were blessed with, but with one of each, we couldn't have wished for better.

The baby was lifted by the midwife onto Jessica's tummy for a first cuddle.

It had started earlier that morning when, already three days past her due date, Jessica had complained of abdominal pains. I'd looked at her as though she was mad. 'So that'll be you in labour, then?' I teased her. She insisted that it wasn't, as it didn't feel the same as the early stages of labour with Harry. I shrugged my shoulders and we got on with our respective activities; Jessica with her feet up on the sofa and a copy of Daphne du Maurier's *Frenchman's Creek* and me working on a website proposal for a client in the first-floor third bedroom used by us both as an office.

A few hours later, Jessica conceded defeat and called Kingston Hospital, still insisting that it didn't compare to her experience with Harry. Predictably, because hospital staff do not want every woman turning up as soon as the contractions become a little bit uncomfortable, she was told to hang on a bit longer and to call back if the contractions became stronger or more frequent.

After an hour Jessica felt she could take no more, and this time she was allowed to come in to hospital. Her mother, Christine, was at home to look after Harry, armed with a sheet of Jessica's instructions. As I drove Jessica to the hospital I felt a knot of excitement inside me.

Once she'd been checked in and taken to a delivery suite at about two o'clock in the afternoon, Jessica was hooked up to a foetal monitor and we were left alone for half an hour or so to watch television and wait. On her return the midwife examined Jessica and looked at the chart that had been spewing out of the monitor and towards the floor. She started to explain that Jessica was still a long way off and that she should go home. But Jessica let out a cry and begged not to be sent home. Seeing her distress, the midwife agreed to let her stay.

Jessica and I had once spent a happy hour discussing a list of old wives' tales we'd found on the Internet about how to tell what sex your baby is, marking a score against each one. Foetal heart rate is said to be an indicator as well. On one antenatal visit the baby's heart rate was recorded in Jessica's notes and my mother had asked again and again what it was, but we wouldn't let on. She said that if it was over 140 it would be a girl. The heart rate recorded had been 143! On balance the old wives' also pointed to a girl, but Jessica never counted her chickens. It was evident to all that, had Baby been a boy, she would have been equally ecstatic. She was always a brilliant mother, the best. Ask her friends. Ask Harry.

Minutes after the delivery Jessica said to me, 'Now I've got my perfect family!' Then, after a pause, she added, looking at me with her Labrador eyes: 'Can I stop now?' I hugged her. It was such a Percy thing to say. I was so proud of her. We were so happy – a wonderful three-year-old son and now a beautiful daughter for Jessica to clothe in pretty dresses and play dolls with. The future looked fantastic. We had everything we had ever wanted. As Laura, my sister, said to me on the telephone later on when I rang from the hospital car park, 'A designer family'. Nothing could go wrong now. We felt we were invincible.

```
From: Minette Palmer
To: Multiple addresses
Date: 24 June 2004 20:39
Subject: Midsummer baby

Dear All,
Just to let you know that Ben and Jessica had
a baby girl this evening, 9lb 13oz, dark hair,
no name yet. Mother and babe both very well.
Lots of love,
Minette xxx
```

Later in the evening, having ensured that both Jessica and our daughter were settled in the maternity ward, I went home – exhausted, but over the moon.

```
From: Ralph Lucas
To: Minette Palmer
Date: 24 June 2004 22:03
Subject: Midsummer baby

Pass on congratulations and sympathy - must
have been one huge push!
Ralph
```

Meeting Jessica

On Friday, 12 February 1993 I was at a loose end.

'I'm meeting Andrew and Graham in the Hollywood Arms. Why don't you come and join us?' asked my cousin, Ed, on the telephone in the early evening.

'I'll see you there,' I told him.

Little did I know that a quiet drink (inasmuch as any Friday night in the pub was quiet, back in our twenties when carefree weekends meant late nights, lie-ins and breakfast at the greasy-spoon café) would so dramatically change the course of my life.

Pushing past crowded tables and a two-deep line at the bar, I located Ed and the others at the back of the noisy pub. I pulled up a stool and someone went to get a fresh round of drinks. The evening was a typical Friday night wind-down; we weren't particularly talent spotting, as we might sometimes have done.

A couple of rounds into the evening, Andrew started talking about his recent exploit, Saving the Whale, and I had to stifle a yawn. Don't get me wrong – it's a totally admirable cause, but while he was talking I was thinking about a holiday to Cape Cod, New England when, together with the family friends I'd been staying with, I had taken a day's boat ride off the coast to watch whales. Aged only twelve, I was fascinated by the experience, watching the whales jump, roll and blow, pointing and laughing with admiration along with my friend Zander and his younger sister (who, like mine, was called Laura). I snapped photos of the whales happily with my simple camera, and only later discovered the disappointment of capturing a whale after it had jumped and was below water again.

I never saw Zander again. We grew up on opposite sides of the pond, and on the one occasion he came to London in early adult life with a college rowing eight, I was out of town. A short while after that he was tragically killed on his way to a fishing expedition when the light aircraft he was a passenger in crashed into the side of a mountain in low cloud.

Brought back to the present, and realising that I was bored, I offered to buy another round. I squeezed my way to the end of the bar and, as I waited my turn to catch the barman's eye and get my order in, I scanned the opposite end of the pub where I caught sight of another group of friends.

They were my more regular crowd of weekend pub companions. There was Henry Harries who was in my house at school, known affectionately as Jabba to his mates, due to a supposed resemblance in his early teens to Jabba the Hutt from the *Star Wars* films. Calling him by that name was once guaranteed to get you a punch in the ribs, but it had stuck. As I looked about to see who else was there, I noticed a new face – long, brown hair and large, dark, smiling eyes. She was wearing a black leather jacket and she smiled when she turned and caught my look. She was lovely.

I paid for the drinks and delivered them to the table before making my excuses. 'I'm going over to say "Hi" to Jabba,' I told Ed. Pushing, squeezing and apologising my way through the pub, I got to the fruit machines in the screened area beside the door and found that my friends were playing a pub quiz game.

'Bezza!' Henry greeted me with a friendly punch to the arm. 'You'd better be good at this.'

I positioned myself next to the leather jacket and joined in the heated argument about correct answers.

She was shorter than I was, but enormous in personality. With her biker jacket she wore dark red jeans and brown leather ankle-length boots, the type with a metal ring near the bottom. She was drinking from a pint glass, yet she was so feminine and bubbly with a sparkle in her eyes. I thought she was totally gorgeous.

'I'm Percy,' she told me over her shoulder as we continued to call out answers to the quiz. She was 'Percy' (short for Percival, her surname) to her friends, 'Jessica' to her family and 'Jess' to her work colleagues. She didn't like being called Jess, but was used to it. She much preferred to be known as Percy.

'Ben. Bezza to this lot,' I said into her ear, over the noise.

Several times the back of her shoulder pressed into my chest. Partly, it was the pushing and jostling of the crowd around us; partly, it was us. Neither of us moved away too quickly.

All too soon, the landlord rang his bell for closing time and a move to a club – Crazy Larry's – was suggested. We all spilled out of the pub and Percy offered a lift in her car. It was a 'handed-down-from-her-mother' blue and white Citroën 2CV, with a mossy canvas roof that leaked in the rain. Joss – an old school friend – Jabba and I piled in after Percy, someone else squeezed in as well somehow, and we crossed Fulham.

The club was crowded and so Joss and Percy agreed to my idea of a quieter drink back at the dilapidated corner town house where I was then living (in exchange for doing some decorating prior to its sale). It overlooked the grass and tennis courts in front of the Royal Hospital Chelsea and was a short hop from my Fulham stamping ground.

After a while, Joss got bored and left the house, leaving Percy and I chatting away like we'd known each other for years. Eventually,

Percy made a move to leave as well, so I got up. We kissed. I held her slight frame in my arms and felt carefree and happy. 'Stay the night?' I suggested through Dutch courage. Slightly tempted, she then recoiled, 'No! I can't. My mother. I . . .' She gave me her home telephone number and I kissed her goodnight.

The following morning, I looked at the number written on a scrap of paper and thought about calling it. Too soon? Too keen? Was she really interested? Several times during the course of the day I picked up the telephone and replaced it. Finally, mid-afternoon I dialled. 'May I speak to Percy, please?' The seconds ticked by like minutes before she came on the line. We arranged to meet up later, and I smiled. I was happy, glad not to have been rebuffed. How little I knew!

She came over later in the afternoon, and we went together to dinner at Joss's brother Alex's house in West Hampstead. After dinner, Percy drove us back to Chelsea, where we chatted, laughed and cuddled. It felt like we had known each other for ever. We explored the house together, and I showed her the rickety lift carved through the centre of the house that the now deceased mother of the house's owner had needed to get from top to bottom. I showed her the cramped 1950s-style kitchen, the quirky Formica-covered bathrooms and the view from my attic room.

This time she stayed the night with no protestations. Both of us were in a whirlwind. In the morning Percy admitted to me that she had waited the day before within earshot of the telephone, wishing – willing – me to call.

The thirteenth of February became the date that we counted as the official 'start' of our relationship, and one that we always celebrated as much as the next day, St Valentine's.

After the weekend I was due to go to West Sussex for the week to help a friend who was working on a Royal College of Art student production of *The Miller's Tale* as an Art Department Assistant. I don't know quite how I got roped in, but they were a fun crowd and while there was no pay, food and board were provided and it was something new to do. I promised Percy that I'd see her the following weekend, and drove myself and a couple of the crew down to the Weald and Downland Open Air Museum of historic houses where filming was due to start. It was a lively, young crew – mostly unpaid except for a handful of professional actors: Vincent Regan, Charlotte Randle and Ken Parry (who always had a story about playing in the BBC's *Children's Hospital*). It was hard work but a great laugh. We were all, some thirty odd, billeted in an empty seven-bedroom house where we slept, three or four to a room, on the floor in sleeping bags – there wasn't a stick of furniture.

Midweek, I was chatting to some of the make-up and costume girls, saying how I was going to head back on Friday to see my girlfriend. 'Bring her down here,' they said. 'Everyone else's boy/girlfriends are coming. It'll be fun.' Convinced that she'd be welcome, even if she'd have to help out, I called Percy and suggested it. Equally persuaded, she agreed to get a train after work on Friday night. I would drive her back to London in my Golf on Monday morning, in time for work. I was elated; I really had a girlfriend and was proud to say so.

Friday night came and I drove to the nearby train station. But there was no Jessica. This can't be right, I thought to myself. I was sure she'd wanted to come and that she did like me. Didn't she? I couldn't have been stood up like this. I waited and waited, then called her mother's house. 'Mrs Percival? It's Ben. Percy is coming, isn't she?' Worried, Percy's mum replied that yes, she was, and she confirmed the train times. 'Maybe she missed the train; I'll wait,' I told her, promising to call back.

After a while I heard a familiar voice and saw Percy crossing over the footbridge. I'd only been waiting on the wrong side of the track, leaving her to think that she was the one that had been stood up on a dark platform in the middle of nowhere. We kissed, both glad to be together. Then Percy called her mother, and we drove back to the house.

It was a fun weekend of long hours and hard work, but Percy mucked in and got on with everyone. We dressed fake window frames, plucked a dead pheasant to put on the set's dining-room table and covered a cobbled road with 'rotting' vegetables and horse manure before sweeping it all up again after the scene was filmed and the camera gate was checked, as all the while we tried to keep a curious viewing public out of camera shot.

One of the girls, Laura in wardrobe, commented to me that Percy and I looked good together. 'How long have you been going out with her?' she asked me, her jaw dropping when I said it was just seven days. 'But you've been here for five of those seven!' Laura laughed. 'She's a good girl, and she must like you a lot. I hope you'll be very happy together.'

In one break, Percy and I sat on a picnic bench eating sandwiches and drinking Diet Coke. We were finding out about each other – checking for chequered pasts and slowly letting our guards down. 'For all I know, you've got children,' she laughed.

I went a bit quiet. 'I nearly did have,' I confessed. She looked at me quizzically. There was no getting out of this one now. 'It was an accident,' I told her. 'It wasn't a serious thing, and she only told me after she'd had a termination. I'm sure it was for the best.' The childhood Catholic in me wasn't entirely comfortable with it, coming from a still strong anti-abortion stance, but Percy was sweet about this early shared secret.

The following day – Sunday – the two of us went to church. So did the rest of the cast and crew, their generator truck, lights, cameras, sound equipment and regalia. Chaucer's parson was in the pulpit holding forth about lasciviousness and, if you watch the tape, you can just make out Percy and me sitting in a back row in headscarves and smocks playing part of a sleepy congregation.

Make or Break

Back in London, Percy and I were happy and inseparable for several months, much to the chagrin of Jabba, with whom I was now sharing a small house in Parson's Green. He didn't much appreciate Jessica's continual presence and, increasingly, he spent time at his girlfriend's flat. But I missed the laddish camaraderie too. Percy's once welcome affections were beginning to feel clingy, and I didn't really know how to balance the two sides of my life. I had become a bit distant and aloof with her, and one weekend morning I called Percy at home. 'Can I come over?' I asked her.

'Why?' she wanted to know. I wasn't going to end our relationship over the telephone but she heard it in my voice. 'Are you going to chuck me?' her voice faltered.

'Best I come over and we have a chat.'

When I got to Percy's mother's jasmine-covered house in Kew, I rang the bell. Kit answered the door. Kit, or Christopher, Percy's younger brother, is quiet – monosyllabic, at best. He does, though, possess an overwhelming knowledge of London's buses, and can direct you from anywhere to anywhere. Brain-damaged at birth, Kit is in a grey area somewhere between severe learning disabled and normal (if there is such a thing) and has mild Asperger's, but he was always immensely fond of his big sister. Jessica, in return, loved him dearly and never made excuses or allowances for him. She would simply say, 'He's the only brother I've ever had, and that makes him normal as far as I'm concerned.' Kit spent most of his time at a Camphill Community centre in Gloucestershire, where he thrived. Percy and I used to make fudge (with mixed results) to sell on a stall at their open-day fête.

Jessica and Kit (when he was in London) lived with Christine – their mother – and their black cat, Tiger, in an end-of-terrace house, with a small but well loved and perfectly tended garden with a fish pond. Christine and Tim, her ex-husband, had divorced when Jessica was in her mid-teens. Christine had taken the children to live with her youngest sister in Blackheath at first, eventually buying the house in Kew.

'Hello, Kit,' I said. 'Can I talk to Percy?'

She came out and we walked around the block, slowly. There wasn't a lot I could say, other than, 'Yes, I am ending it,' as Percy protested and questioned – I had little in the way of constructive argument. I wasn't going to back down though, and it wasn't going to be a comfortable walk back to the house. Mostly, there was silence, but I could feel Percy's anger. We got back to her front door, and I took a couple of her things out of my car: boots and a map. She walked up the short front path, partly obscured from my view by lavender bushes. She stood at the front door, key-less, waiting to be let in again. As I got into my car I heard a cry, a wail almost, that made the hair on the back of my neck stand up; I can still hear it ringing in my ears after fourteen years.

We had no contact for a few weeks, until one evening when I was in Finch's on the Fulham Road, once again drinking with Jabba, Joss, his brother Alex and a few others. I spotted Percy across the pub, sitting with her friends. I desperately wanted to go and talk to her, and confided in Alex that I regretted what I'd done. Thinking it was 'beer talk' he restrained me and convinced me not to do anything, but I knew that I had been stupid, immature and above all else, extremely unkind; and look at her – she was so vivacious and pretty.

On my next weekend visit to my parents in Hampshire, I spoke frankly to my mother one evening, confessing: 'I've made the biggest mistake of my life.'

A week or so after this, I heard on the grapevine that Percy was meeting Jason – one of our regular Friday- and Saturday-night gang members – for an early-evening drink after work at the White Horse, and that, probably unbeknown to her, he had designs. My mind was made up in an instant. I knew I had to rectify my mistake before it was too late. I rang my cousin, Ed, and told him that I needed him to meet me for a quiet drink and that we would accidentally bump into Jessica. He would spot her first.

I left Ed sitting at a wrought-iron table in the pavement garden and went in for drinks. When I returned and put the drinks down I sat with my back to where Jessica was sitting with Jason on the other side of the garden. My heart pounding, I indicated to Ed that he should spot them now. He played it perfectly, and soon we were all sitting around their table together, cramping Jason's style enormously. Ed engaged Jason and I started chatting to Jessica, catching up on the weeks that had passed. Bored and disillusioned, first Jason and then Ed – his services no longer required – made their excuses and left.

Suddenly feeling nervous and ill at ease, I told Percy that I had bought a van. A big white transit van. What a chat-up line! But she did express an interest in coming to see it. Over the previous few years, I had been decorating, originally for friends of my parents and family, slowly progressing to heavier jobs, carpentry, plastering and other repairs. I'm not quite sure how I started on this road; it just took on its own momentum as I acquired new skills through a combination of necessity and working alongside others. My Golf was soon too small to carry the tools and materials that I needed, and was slowly getting dirtier and shabbier than it had once been. The car was a second-hand 21st-birthday present and, when I decided to buy a van, Mum took first refusal and bought the car back off me for my siblings to learn to drive in. I greatly enjoyed haggling between two or three commercial vehicle dealers and eventually bought a short wheel base Ford Transit, with a semi-high roof. I was amused at being White Van Man. My friends always wanted to know how many copies of the Sun were stuffed onto the dashboard, and whether I knew where the indicators were.

We found ourselves going for a 'test drive'.

'Where shall we go?' I asked Percy, but she didn't know. We drove out of Fulham; I desperately wanted to talk to her – properly – but didn't know where to start, so we kept on driving. Up the Fulham Palace Road, into the Hammersmith roundabout and on towards Chiswick. The traffic was light and it was still warm in the evening sunshine. With the windows wound down, we agreed to go for a road trip. I hadn't the faintest idea where to, but as we were already headed towards the M4, I thought of Windsor. I knew it well, having been to school at Eton, on the other side of the Thames.

I still didn't know how to start saying what was burning inside me as I parked beside the river. I suggested we walk. We crossed over the Windsor footbridge, passed the boathouses and went along the towpath in the evening sun, following the river where I had sculled so many times in the past. We walked under the 'Motorway' bridge – as we had called it at school, even though it carries an 'A' road – around the right-hand bend, past the long meadow grass and then we crossed the arched wooden bridge over a side water, pausing to watch the swans glide past. A little further on there was a bench. We sat down together and huddled into our too thin clothes against the falling chill. It was make-or-break time. If I didn't speak now I knew I may not have the opportunity again.

'What would you do if you knew you'd made a mistake and didn't know what to do about it?' I asked.

Percy was bemused.

'Well, if you actually liked someone, but didn't know how to start to tell them,' I went on. But I wasn't getting the message across. Percy was very quiet, which wasn't helping.

In the end I blurted out, 'I finished things between us for what I thought were the right reasons, but I miss you, and I know that I shouldn't have done it. I regret it and I'm sorry.'

She was dumbfounded. 'I was about to hit you,' she told me. 'I thought you were asking my advice about another girlfriend. And to think that I was nearly over you! Do you mean it?'

I did, and cautiously we hugged and kissed. I knew I was happy again. We walked back, retracing our steps, but with our arms around each other this time. We paused on the wooden bridge to play Pooh-sticks, and kissed again. We held hands in the van, driving back to London in the dark.

With hindsight, we both agreed that the break was, although unkind, a wholesome feature of our relationship, as we reconvened on a much better and stronger footing. Eventually, we stopped counting it and the split was lost in time.

The Flat

At the end of our year's rental period on the house in Parson's Green, Henry and I amicably moved our separate ways and I rented a first-floor flat in Woodlawn Road, near Bishop's Park, from the son of a friend of my maternal grandmother.

In early 1994 I decided to buy a flat with help from my parents and a mortgage making up the difference. I liked the area I was in and so looked locally. Most of the flats were out of my price bracket, but I found a ground-floor flat in Langthorne Street that was slightly cheaper than average, but close to the park and the River Thames. The flat needed a lot of renovation, but it was in a nice house and had a decent-sized, unplanted garden. Sometimes when you drove down the street you would see a sailing boat's mast passing the end of the road, and as the river itself wasn't visible this sight had a surreal quality.

I spent a lot of my working time with a plumber with whom I got on well and who had taught me a great deal about the trade. With his help, I was planning to move the kitchen from the middle of the flat to the rear bedroom, which led out into the garden, and to replace the bathroom, boiler and central heating system. The work would take about four to six weeks, working around our other jobs. Jessica had taken over the rental of the Woodlawn Road flat, and so we shared it and the limited cupboard space until I could move in.

I took possession of the flat on a warm June day, and was incredibly excited. I opened my front door and walked through the flat. With no furniture or curtains it seemed much more desolate than I had remembered and dirt showed around the edges of where pictures had hung. I looked into the kitchen and was glad it would soon be ripped out as it was cramped, with very tired wall and floor units. Then, I went to look out of the window, and standing where the fridge had stood, I noticed the wall at my knee level. The plasterboard was bubbled and stained, so I prodded it. My hand went more or less straight through and on into the bathroom with very little effort. A hundred thoughts raced through my head in a flash, but I felt cheated and conned, very angry and stupid to have bought a total lemon. Quite why a small amount of water damage from the bath mattered when the two rooms were going to be stripped back almost to brick in any case, I do not know. I just wanted it to be perfect, and I was angry with myself for not having noticed the damage.

By the time the flat was refitted, working around my other projects, I was exhausted. I was also becoming tired and disillusioned by the long hours with early starts and back-breaking work, followed by paperwork in the evenings, doing job costings and quotations.

Using paints, chemicals, cement and plaster was also causing continual skin irritation. My GP prescribed a steady stream of steroid and barrier creams, but once remarked 'Isn't there another career you could follow?' I started to think that maybe that wasn't such a bad idea.

Jessica had, before and after going to university, worked for a classic

car auction house, Coys of Kensington as Auction Administrator. One day, she came home and told me that their computer support man was becoming slower and slower to respond to their requests for help, and that they had a problem. 'For goodness sake,' Jessica had said in the office, 'my boyfriend could fix this quicker than he can.'

'Well get him in then,' her boss told her. So this was my introduction to classic cars and information technology as a career, and for several years Jessica and I worked alongside each other at Coys. Much as I had with building work, I learned my skills through demand and the fledgling World Wide Web. In time, Jessica moved on to work for other classic car auction and sales companies, but I continued working freelance for Coys, as well as other clients who needed a database, website or new computer network, many of which were also classic car businesses. It is a competitive but close-knit industry.

Day 2:
Friday, 25 June

From: Liz Bryant
To: Minette Palmer
Date: 25 June 2004 06:58
Subject: Midsummer baby

Thank you so much for letting us know - and
congratulations to parents, grandparents,
aunts, uncles and anyone else who feels glowing pride in the event!
Simon and I hope to be at Temple on the 11th
- so may see you then.
Have fun with it all.
Liz

```
From: David Legh
To: Minette Palmer
Date: 25 June 2004 08:02
Subject: Re: Midsummer baby


Congratulations! Please give very best wishes
to both happy parents. Big girl!
Lol
David and Jane


From: Anthea Palmer
To: Minette Palmer
Date: 25 June 2004 08:21
Subject: Midsummer baby


How lovely. Are they still at the same ad-
dress in Southfields?
Love to hear when you know a name.
CONGRATULATIONS GRANNY!!!!!!!!!
Love from Anthea
```

In the morning, Jessica telephoned me at home from the television/
telephone device beside her hospital bed, saying that she and the
baby would be discharged at ten o'clock. Thrilled, I dropped three-
year-old Harry off at his nursery for half-past nine and drove straight
to the hospital.

When I arrived on the ward, Jessica was gloomy. 'My blood pressure was low, then they took it again and it was normal, but they might
not let me out just yet.' She looked so tired. She told me that Baby
had been crying for food all night, and that she had only managed
to get one hour's sleep.

The sister came over to us with a bottle of milk for Baby, to top
her up and take some of the pressure off of Jessica. Then she started

to discuss the blood pressure issue and Jessica was not at all happy that she wasn't going home there and then. An anaesthetist came to see her, to check she didn't have any post-epidural side effects, and the sister asked her to check Jessica's blood pressure, explaining about the previous contradictory readings. The anaesthetist was not pleased to be asked to do this – she may have thought it a job below her station. She did check it, however, then said that Jessica was borderline tachy-cardic. I think she was surprised the sister hadn't realised. And they both commented that she was looking a little flushed as well.

Jessica complained and protested, saying she was only flushed because she felt hot from the waterproof mattress protector and that the best thing for her was to go home for some rest. She could be quite determined when her mind was made up and she repeated her argument several times. However, they agreed that there was no way Jessica should leave, although she could discharge herself. I assured them that I wouldn't let that happen; I would overrule. She wasn't leaving until they were entirely happy for her to do so, much as we both wanted us all to be at home together.

I took Baby for a walk along the corridors in her hospital cot, to allow Jessica some sleep. I think she managed about 45 minutes to an hour while I wheeled Baby up and down and rocked the cot to try and settle her, but she would not stop crying.

A midwife passed me and said, 'Pick her up and rock her in your arms. Just don't sit down. They like it when you're standing up, and they do know!'

She was absolutely right, of course. The moment I tried to sit down with her, Baby would start crying.

'Rock me until your arms ache and your legs are numb,' I think she was saying. I stood and watched banal daytime television, rocking her all the while. Anything I can do for you is fine, my little one, I thought. I love you.

I collected Harry from nursery and gave him some lunch at home. After his rest, we drove to the hospital, chatting animatedly in the car. We bought juice and snacks from the shop inside the main hospital entrance on the way in and, full of excitement, we walked to Jessica's room. As we had arranged, I peeped around the curtain pulled across her bed and signalled for her to put Baby down so as not to make Harry feel sidelined.

Jessica welcomed Harry with open arms. 'I've missed you so much, Harry,' she said. 'I hear you've been such a good boy!'

Harry embraced her while looking over his shoulder at the small, blanketed bundle. 'Is that my baby, Mummy?' he asked. 'Will she want to play with me?' His curiosity and pride ran as high as his expectations of her.

We'd hoped to drive home together, all four of us, as a family. But it wasn't to be. After an hour or so of telling Jessica what we'd been doing at home, what he had done at nursery school that day, and having eaten his snacks, Harry grew tired and irritable in the warmth of the ward. There was still no sign of a doctor to see Jessica and hopefully to discharge her, so, downhearted, Harry and I headed home for his tea.

At around eight o'clock, I left Harry at home with Christine, who'd come over for that purpose as she had done the day before, and returned to the hospital to find that Jessica had been discharged by the doctor, who had finally turned up. She'd be ready to leave as soon as they had printed the letters to midwife, GP and health visitor.

'Where have you been?' she asked me. 'I've been ringing.' I explained that I had left as soon as I could after getting Harry to bed, and before I'd heard that they were ready to come home. She was cross and short-tempered. We said our goodbyes to the staff then I packed Jessica and Baby into the car and brought them home. We were all worn out, but now elated to be finally home and together.

After a steak, baked potato and salad for supper, which Christine kindly cooked for us all, but of which Jessica ate little, she suddenly became very tired and started shaking. It seemed that everything had caught up with her, so I helped her up to bed. When we got upstairs, she was cold and shivery and her lips were blue. She checked on her sleeping baby, beside our bed – in the same Moses basket that Harry had used – then climbed into bed, fully dressed.

'Come on, silly, you can't go to sleep in your clothes,' I told her. I helped her to get changed and into bed where she soon warmed up and started to feel better. Only a bit too hot to the touch now, I thought. I took her temperature using a digital thermometer and was alarmed; it was nearly 40°C. 'Shouldn't we call someone?' I asked, concerned about her state.

'Fuck off. Let me go to sleep. I'm so tired. I didn't sleep last night. I'll be fine.'

Don't argue with a pregnant or hormonal woman; and certainly not when she's sleep deprived. Years of experience had taught me that. So I told Jessica that if she felt at all unwell in the night I would call an ambulance for her. Then I checked on Harry next door, tucking him up in his junior cot bed before retreating back downstairs.

As far as I know – being fast asleep throughout the night myself – Jessica slept soundly, bar the night feeds. Our young family was just tired from the excitement. Everything would be all right in the morning, wouldn't it?

Proposal and Marriage

After a false start a year or so earlier, when I had nearly plucked up courage to ask Tim for Jessica's hand in marriage – over a pint in a quiet country pub – by the New Year of 1999 I knew that I couldn't imagine not spending the rest of my life with his daughter. We had been together for nearly six years and to some of our friends it seemed as though we were already married.

In early February I visited an old-fashioned, family-run jeweller's in Gloucester Road, around the corner from Coys where I was still working, and told them what I was looking for. Perusing a tray of rings I had a good idea of what I wanted, but didn't see it at first. Then they brought out a single ring – it was not new, but sparkled as bright as any I had already seen and was much more what I had in mind. Slender and delicate, with three diamonds set in white gold, I could see it on Jessica's finger and had to have it.

It didn't quite cost the month's salary that I believe is the amount a man might well spend, but it was perfect and I felt sure that Jessica would have chosen it herself – except that I wanted the surprise to be complete.

I kept the ring hidden away in my sock drawer for a few days before going out to buy red roses and a red heart-shaped helium balloon, which I stuffed into the wardrobe before Jessica came home on Saturday, 13 February, six years – almost to the day – after we had met.

As we relaxed together on the sofa, each with a glass of wine, my nerves were all over the place; I knew it was now or never. I was terrified that she might turn me down, but I sat up and looked at her. 'Close your eyes,' I told her.

'Why?'

'Just trust me and close them,' I said, as I nipped to the bedroom next door to collect the flowers, balloon and ring box. I placed the vase of roses on the floor in front of her, with the balloon's ribbon tied around it, then knelt down on one knee in front of her with the ring behind my back. 'Open your eyes,' I said to Jessica.

She looked at me with wide eyes and opened her mouth to speak.

'Will you marry me?' I cut her short.

For one moment Jessica was uncharacteristically speechless, and it felt like an age before she said, 'Yes. Of course I will, you fool. I thought you'd never ask. I just thought you'd remembered our anniversary.'

I had never felt so safe, loved and wanted as we hugged and laughed. She loved the ring and it was a perfect fit on her slender finger.

'What do we do next?' she asked me.

'I don't know – I've never been engaged. Maybe we tell everyone!'

We couldn't get hold of Tim and Marian on the telephone, but the next morning we 'dropped' in on Christine. 'I knew that's why you'd come,' she said with delight after we told her, and she congratulated us again before we set off for Hampshire to tell my parents. We rang them from a pub car park on the outskirts of Farnham, thinking we'd have a bite to eat before another drop-in after lunch.

'Where are you? Can you come for lunch?' Mum asked. So, with Plan 'A' out of the window, we walked into their kitchen half an hour later.

'We've got some news,' I said to my parents. 'Last night I asked Percy to marry me.'

There was a pregnant pause full of inquisitive looks, before Jessica put them out of their misery with: 'And I said yes!'

I think Mum would have cried had she not asked my father, Papa, if he had any champagne. We couldn't have been any happier or more excited. Laura was also at home for the weekend and she too was almost in tears. After a moment, while the news sank in, she suddenly squealed, 'Oh my God, Percy. You're going to be Mrs Palmer. That's so funny!'

The following day, Sunday, we drove to Marlow for tea where, to our relief, we found Tim and Marian. We hadn't been able to get hold of them by telephone, so had gambled on their being away until early evening. They were somewhat taken aback to see us, despite the cryptic message we'd left on their answerphone, particularly as first I, and then Jessica, walked into the room literally shaking with nerves and excitement.

'Tim, I hope you'll forgive the lack of protocol, but I've asked Jessica to marry me and—'

'I said yes!' blurted Jessica – her enthusiasm clear once again, as was the delight in both their faces.

The wedding machine quickly spun into action. In a short space of time Christine had found a caterer, florist and photographer. We also learned that because she worked in the House of Commons we were entitled to be married at St Margaret's Westminster, known as 'the parish church of the House of Commons'. I was particularly pleased as I discovered that my father's mother, Granny, and my aunt had both been married there many years before. Even so, we had to apply for a signed and sealed special licence from the Archbishop of Canterbury.

The reception was to be held in the City, at Mercers' Hall, as both my father and I are liverymen or members of the Mercers' Company – the senior of the City Livery Companies – as are most of the men, and now women, in our family. The hall has a grand entrance and beautiful reception rooms, in some of which hang portraits of my ancestors. Jessica was delighted.

The planning involved several lunches between in-laws – which, with three sets, in itself involves some planning – but all the meetings were happy and excited affairs, except for one at which we had gathered to swap notes on some specifics of the wedding plans.

Jessica and I had wanted to keep a degree of control over the wedding. 'It's my day; they've had theirs,' she told me once, obviously not wanting to wait until her day as mother of the bride. I pointed out to her, with a cheeky smile, that it was 'our' day, and promised it would be the way she wanted! One of the things we had talked about was whether or not to have a wedding list. Jessica's instinct was not to, but I could foresee a dozen toasters and fifteen rugs if we didn't. So, we agreed that we would have one, but that we would try to present it in as un-grabbing a way as possible. We both knew it would be contentious with our parents.

When we sat down with our files after lunch at Christine's house we swapped guest-list updates and menus and I showed them the printed invitations, divided up according to Jessica's strict parental guest allowance. Then the gift list came up. Almost in unison our mothers said, 'You're not going to say you've got a list with the invitations are you?' There was an uproar. I told them that we were happy to talk about it but that ultimately it was our decision. Once more, I was shouted down.

Then Jessica spoke up. She said that we had already debated and discussed it and that our choice was to go with it, whether popular or not. This was my first real taste of the unity of marriage and I loved it. I loved Jessica and could have hugged her for this show of support.

(Of course, when they sent their invitations out, our parents cut off the mention of a list at the bottom of the accompanying sheet of maps and directions!)

On the eve of our wedding day Jessica went over to her mother's house and my best man, Tim Schofield, came to my flat. I told Jessica that he and I were taking her British racing green MGB GT to her father's house in Marlow so that it would be safe during our honeymoon. Quite why that made sense, I'm not sure, but it meant that it totally threw Jessica off the scent as to where we were honey-mooning. She didn't want to know where we were going, just what clothes she should take.

Tim and I collected the three tiers of our wedding cake from a wonderful family business in Kew and drove car, luggage and cake up to Mercers' Hall and garaged it next to the stacked boxes of my soon-to-be father-in-law's wine and champagne. We then caught a taxi back to Fulham, and each went back to our flats to change for the evening. My little flat seemed very strange without Jessica there and the feeling that I wouldn't see her again in this single life was somehow worrying.

Tim and I ate and drank well at Chutney Mary's on the King's Road before returning to my flat to finish writing and rehearsing our speeches. I found it hard to relax and stayed up late into the night.

Up bright and early in the morning, we each dressed in our morning coats and went by taxi to Claridge's for breakfast. This was Tim's treat – a really generous gesture – but he was disappointed that we weren't allowed a champagne breakfast as licensing laws forbade the sale of alcohol to non-residents at that time of morning.

Nevertheless, we ate smoked salmon and scrambled eggs, somewhat more reluctantly in my case because my stomach was in a total knot from nerves. The coffee, however, was good and strong.

When our taxi dropped us on Parliament Square, beside the entrance to St Margaret's, at about quarter to eleven for the eleven-thirty service, we found it still locked. As my brothers, cousin and Kit (the ushers) arrived we managed to get the attention of a verger to let us in. Jessica's white standard marguerite daisies had been arranged at the front of the church and the sun was shining in through a stained-glass window. With very little wedding dressing the church was magnificent and welcoming, but still quiet.

Then the seats began to fill with smiling guests and the organist played chamber music in the background. I spied Granny walking up the aisle looking unsure as to where she should sit. I went up to meet her and offered to take her to her reserved seat. She was taken aback at receiving such service: 'I didn't expect the groom to show me to my seat,' she sparkled.

'Nothing less, Granny,' I told her and led her to her place, before taking up my own position.

As the organist played the first notes of 'The Prince of Denmark's March', I turned to the end of the aisle to see Jessica. She was absolutely stunning as she walked towards me on Tim's arm in an ivory dress with bell-shaped sleeves and a full veil. Tim, for his part, was in his clan kilt and walking with his inimitable gait, caused in no small part by a succession of rugby injuries and operations. As I looked at Jessica I had a lump in my throat and tears of pride pricked my eyes.

My heart was pounding as we sang, 'Be thou my vision, O Lord of my Heart'. My God, she was my vision that day. As we made our vows to each other, there was nobody else in the church as far as we were concerned. They had all become shrouded in a mist around us. I was barely even aware of Canon Wright's voice as we repeated words after him. When I carefully lifted back Jessica's veil and kissed her, I felt I was the happiest I could ever have been.

Then we sat down and I caught sight of my family behind us, tears of happiness in their eyes. 'It can't be that bad,' I wanted to joke, but instead I just smiled at them.

After the service, Jessica and I led bridesmaids, page, best man and family back down the aisle to the door, pausing halfway for a posed photograph. Jessica put one hand through my arm and rested it in my elbow, holding her enormous bouquet in her left. There was jostling behind us, and I muttered to Jessica through a fixed smile, 'I wish the photographer would hurry up.' We posed again with parents and wedding party on the church steps, then everyone was free to pour out of the church onto the path and lawns.

We were all milling about amid calls of congratulations when someone pointed out that the railings on Parliament Square were literally hung with tourists, all clamouring for a better view. Because St Margaret's is right next to Westminster Abbey, they must have believed us to be among the rich and famous, a theory that was fuelled when one of our friends let word get out that we were a duke and duchess. That, of course, sent the Japanese into a frenzy of flash photography. Many a time we laughed afterwards about the poor people who had added our pictures to their holiday albums, convinced that they had an exclusive.

Jessica and I were driven by our friend, ex-boss and client, Chris, in a most elegant 1925 Hispano Suiza, borrowed from Coys where he was Sales Director, along the Embankment and through the City to Mercers' Hall, while our guests were transported in a combination of limousines, black cabs and an open-top double-decker bus, hired by Jessica.

After the formal photographs had been taken, Jessica and I joined our friends and family in the big hall, and were totally swept up in hugs, kisses and congratulations with barely a moment to speak to each other. At one point somebody wanted to ask Jessica something, but she was nowhere to be seen. I remember moving from room to room looking for her, saying, 'I've lost my wife.' It felt strange to call her that, so I said it again, and loved it. My wife. When I did eventually find her, she was sitting on the floor, playing with her page and bridesmaids.

Lunch was a fantastic buffet spread, but Jessica and I could barely touch it we were so excited and happy. After lunch the Mercers' Beadle – resplendent in tails and red sash – called order, and we prepared to cut the cake. Jessica and I held the knife together, my arm around her waist. Being wedded was such bliss; I was already wondering why I hadn't done it years earlier.

All too soon, it was the moment I had been dreading. I hate public speaking, and was terrified of making my speech. John Gordon, an old family friend of the Percivals spoke first, but in my nervousness most of his words passed me by. The only thing I heard was a reference to my white van. Knowing that my speech also mentioned it, I told him as I was passed the microphone stand that he'd stolen my thunder. Of course he hadn't, but what I didn't appreciate at the time, but – having been to other weddings – I have since realised, was that I could have said anything at all and been greeted by rapturous applause. On your wedding day you can mumble, cry or just plain freeze, and no one is going to slow hand-clap you.

So I started by thanking John for his kind and eloquent words, and reading from the cards in my palm, I continued: 'When a young man meets a girl, and in due course is invited to meet her parents – over a quiet Sunday lunch for example – he has time to prepare. He buys a bluffer's guide to golf, he practises using a golfing term or two – all in the hope that he doesn't embarrass himself and that he will win their approval.

'It didn't happen like that for me. In July of 1988 at a picnic during Henley Regatta (after a pint or three of Pimms), I met Tim. I had no idea that he might have such an attractive daughter, was consequently "off guard" and probably made a very bad impression.'

'No you didn't!' called Marian from somewhere near the back of the hall. I was surprised to be heckled, but glad it was friendly and supportive.

'It was another four years before I met Jessica through mutual friends and at least another a year again before the photographic evidence of that hot day beside the river was unearthed and that chance meeting remembered. By which time, I think, Tim had even forgiven me for being a non-golfer.'

The rest of my speech seemed to pass by in a flash and when I had thanked and toasted the bridesmaids and page, I stepped down with relief and held Jessica's hand. She smiled and squeezed it.

At around five o'clock we both changed into new clothes and left the reception. The hall's forecourt was crowded with guests and Jessica's MG had been covered in gold streamers and balloons. An imitation American registration plate hung in the back window: 'Just Married. State of Bliss'.

I brought Jessica outside with her eyes closed and when she saw her car, she cried out, 'My baby, my baby,' getting an odd look from someone next to us. As we drove off, I deliberately over-revved the noisy sports exhaust, and we were showered in a hail of durum wheat.

Pregnant with Harry

We'd been married for a little over a year when we stopped trying not to have a baby – we thought, no pressure, take it as it comes. But this quickly became a case of trying to get pregnant, and as the months passed and the more she thought about it, the more Jessica wanted to have a baby.

In late summer 2000, when Jessica's period was overdue, we became very excited. She didn't dare take a pregnancy test for fear of a negative result, but by the time of our friend Vanessa's engagement party we both knew there could be no other reason for the missed period.

'I'll take a test after the party, then I can drink,' Jessica reasoned. 'I'll have to drink or Ness will know, and it's too early for that.' Jessica didn't drink much, but not so little as to raise suspicion – or to her mind, anyway. I'm sure nobody would have given it a second thought if she'd been driving and on fruit juice. She seemed to be glowing during the evening, and we teased and flirted with each other, each of us hoping and willing her to be pregnant.

When we got home, I could no longer control my curiosity and begged Jessica to take the test that had been sitting on top of the shaving light in the bathroom for several days, instead of waiting until the morning. Jessica eventually gave in, laughing at me as she shut me out of the bathroom. I paced the narrow hallway, already feeling very much the expectant father.

When Jessica emerged from the bathroom I thought I saw just the start of a tear in her eye. My heart sank, momentarily. But then she said, 'I'm pregnant!' We laughed and cried and kissed. I had never seen her so happy and so beautiful.

The idea of not telling anyone about the pregnancy until the first three months were up was torture, and I think we caved in to our parents after about six weeks. Jessica went from strength to strength and threw herself into all the preparations, including choosing how she wanted the second bedroom set up as a nursery. She found a plain wooden box for toys, and together we painted it. We cut out teddy bears and balls from a sheet of wrapping paper and glued them on, varnishing it for protection. I bought a copy of *What to Expect When You're Expecting* and read up on everything. Jessica would say, 'I don't want to know yet,' when I got to the gory parts, but together we tracked our baby's growth from raspberry size to grapefruit, and once there was a proper bump, we'd lie in bed and I'd talk to it.

Once, as we were driving in the car, playing Dido loudly, Jessica said, 'Muppet likes Dido, he's dancing!' And so as Dido's words echoed around us, 'Oh I am what I am, I do what I want, But I can't hide . . .' we sang along for the baby, louder and louder.

Never had Jessica done anything so well as she did preparing for our baby, and Muppet rewarded her with very little morning sickness and a straightforward nine months.

On 6 June 2001 Jessica woke me at about half past six in the morning. 'I think it's starting,' she told me. 'I've been having contractions for a couple of hours, and they're definitely not Branston Pickles.' The contractions were mild enough for a fairly normal but quiet day at home, and Jessica kept in contact with the midwives at Queen Charlotte and Chelsea Hospital in Hammersmith. As the pains got stronger and stronger, the TENS machine was less and less effective, and in the evening she was told to come into the hospital.

Labour progressed in fits and starts, and when the gas and air made Jessica throw up for a second time, she asked for an epidural. All night she contracted and neither of us – Jessica in bed, me on a bean bag on the floor – slept for much more than a half-hour stretch. In the early hours she was still a way off, but in pain as the epidural had worn off and she was waiting for a top-up. She sat on the side of her bed rocking and in tears. I felt totally spare and useless, desperately wanting to help. I stood in front of her and stroked her hair as she leaned against my stomach. Once again she started rocking, pummelling my abdomen with the top of her head. It hurt like hell, but what could I say? How many women must wish that childbirth was painful for the father as well? I wasn't going to complain about my discomfort even if I was bruising. Maybe Jessica was transferring some of her pain onto me.

As the morning progressed and baby didn't, the midwives became more and more concerned, and by the time Jessica had been actively pushing for almost two hours a doctor decided to intervene. First, a new and slimmer design of ventouse (then on trial) was used, but to no avail – it just kept popping off the baby's crown. The more cumbersome and traditional version was then wheeled in, with similar results. Jessica was now beside herself and a midwife rushed out to put theatre on standby.

Another doctor came into the delivery room and opened the forceps pack. Sitting between Jessica's stirruped legs he went to work, cutting an episiotomy before pulling on baby with his forceps. When the midwives told Jessica to push and she cried, 'I can't, I can't,' I could see the concern in their faces. On the doctor's firm

35

instruction, I shouted at her as she squeezed the blood out of my hand, 'Push, Percy, you *have* to push.' I had a horrible sense that unless somebody could push or pull our baby out, something was going to go badly wrong.

Finally, the locum paediatrician, who had resisted coming into the delivery room sooner (much to the midwives' annoyance and disbelief), was hauled in to deal with a potential candidate for neo-natal intensive care by a midwife muttering under her breath, 'Someone's going to die unless we have help.'

I don't know who was screaming louder, Jessica or I, as baby emerged in one final push at 11.26 in the morning, and with a clamp and a snip was lifted straight onto a resuscitation trolley.

'It's a boy, Perc, it's a boy – I'm so proud of you. I love you, I love you,' I told her, kissing her forehead. Jessica's wish had come true. She had given me a son. I didn't really care, boy or girl – just that we were a family.

'Why isn't he crying?' Jessica tried to push herself up on her elbows. 'Why isn't my baby crying?' There was a sense of urgency and demand in her voice, but I had no answer and could only look on helplessly, willing somebody to say something as the paediatrician cleared baby's airways with suction and applied an oxygen mask to his tiny and blue face. Time stood still, until our firstborn, our son and heir, let out a piercing scream and the room breathed with him.

Very cautiously, I went over to meet our son. He held my little finger and squeezed; my whole body filled with pride like as though it was given to me intravenously.

When Jessica was stitched and bathed, she was handed our new son, in his blue and white hospital gown, to hold. He was 9lb 4oz and incredibly long. As Jessica cradled him in her arms and he held his mummy's finger, his feet seemed miles away on the bed, to the extent that an orderly queue of midwives had formed to look at the long baby.

As I stood at the window and looked at my wife, my back to the view of HM Prison Wormwood Scrubs, the drama of an hour earlier was brushed aside, and I thought: This was a woman born to be a mother. She held our son so gently, yet so strongly, and she was consumed by love, shattered as she was by a thirty-something hour labour.

Move to Southfields

What with the two of us, Harry and our West Highland terrier, Annie, we were rapidly outgrowing the flat. We considered, but dismissed, a move out of London and, instead, found a terraced house in Southfields. The moment we were shown around the house by its septuagenarian owner, we fell in love with it, seeing past the dated decor and overload of DIY projects. Most important of all, it had a staircase. It was our dream to be able to go upstairs to bed at night, and as we were shown the three bedrooms, we exchanged a knowing look – we were going to buy this place and make it our own.

When moving day came, we said goodbye to the removal lorry in Fulham and gave the flat one last Hoover. Jessica took Harry and Annie in the estate car, to her mother's house in Barnes for the day, while I drove her MG to Southfields for midday and rang the estate agent to find out about getting the keys. Apparently, we hadn't completed and the vendors' solicitor had decided to go out for the afternoon. Although immensely frustrated, there was nothing I could do. The removal men arrived after their lunch stop so we played football in the street and read the papers when we grew tired.

Almost everyone walking past me while I was parked up seemed to be a mother with a pushchair. There was very little traffic, and it looked and felt like our old street in Fulham, just a little bit greener and quieter, and definitely less overhead air traffic. This was home.

I eventually got the keys at five o'clock and the removal men disgorged our boxed world, room by room. They were marvellous and had Harry's nursery unpacked and his cot assembled for us in next to no time. We were finished by half past six. Jessica bathed Harry and settled him down while the rest of us shared two four-packs on the lorry's tailgate.

After they'd left, and having never done it before, I took Jessica outside to the small front garden and carried her over our threshold. This was our new start – a house we'd chosen together, for which we were making plans together and for which both the mortgage and title deeds were in joint names. It felt safe and exciting at the same time.

A week after we moved in it was Harry's first birthday. Harry's friends, mostly children of Jessica's National Childbirth Trust group, godparents, aunts, uncles and grandparents came for a picnic tea on rugs in the garden, and we watched as Harry covered his face in chocolate from his caterpillar cake.

That summer the builders moved in, and Jessica took Harry and Annie down to my parents' house in Hampshire. The kitchen and the adjoining dining-room wall were ripped out, floors levelled and walls plastered. In the evenings I would drive down to Hampshire to see them, and as the new IKEA kitchen was fitted and the whole downstairs was replumbed and rewired I took photographs and video footage to show them. By the time the work was finished we had a modern, functional kitchen with shiny new appliances. It just needed me to decorate it, but we had started to make our mark on the family house.

On the days I wasn't working, over weekends and after Harry had gone to bed, Jessica and I stripped the walls, filled, lined and painted. We worked as a team. Jessica would make sandwiches for lunch and offer words of encouragement when the work seemed neverending and going nowhere. When Harry decided he'd like to climb a ladder or investigate a paint tin, Jessica would take him to the park or to a friend's house. And when we tired of decorating or wanted fresh air, we dug, planted and tended the garden, slowly turning it into her vision. We were very weary at the end of each day and every spare penny seemed to go into house, but we loved seeing our dream coming to fruition. And we loved watching Harry as he grew.

September came and Harry started at nursery school. Jessica had looked into many options and we had visited a few places together, but only one stood out for us. Small, friendly and welcoming, the Gardens Nursery on the first floor of a building above Southfields Club was exactly what we'd had in mind. When he started there Harry was only going to attend for two mornings a week. On his first morning Jessica dropped him off at nine o'clock. He had cried when she left him and she had sat in the car outside for most of the three hours, crying herself. I teased her about it when she told me, though I understood how she missed her baby and felt a wrench at the maternal strings, having spent all of every day with him up until then.

Each day, noon couldn't come soon enough for either of them and Harry (who had been playing quite happily) would burst into tears when he saw his mummy. This pattern repeated itself for the first three weeks, before he realised that he was always collected at the end of the morning, and that he did actually have a lot of fun in the meantime.

The two of them made friends with children and mothers respectively from nursery and soon developed an active local social life, while still keeping up with their Wednesday National Childbirth Trust group lunches. Life in Southfields was treating us well, and we were all happy.

Flying Solo

We hadn't been abroad since our honeymoon, and with reduced income and increased expenditure now that we had a lively and growing two-year-old, we were unlikely to be going anywhere any time soon. However, Christine very kindly invited the three of us to go on holiday with her and a group of friends. It was a very kind offer and it sounded like it would be a fantastic week. We were going to stay in a villa with a pool on Menorca, a short walk from the sea. It would be hot and very relaxing.

Our flights were a couple of hours earlier than the others' as they'd been booked separately but, in any case, the two schedules suited our differing lifestyles. Jessica, Harry and I parked in Gatwick's long-term car park and set about moving Harry, the pushchair and two large suitcases on to a shuttle bus headed for departures.

Thanks to Jessica's great planning and organisational skills, we were in very good time and the check-in queues had barely formed. We pulled the buggy up to the desk, got out tickets and passports, including Harry's brand new one with his little photograph that had been so hard to get him to sit for. The check-in attendant seemed to be taking a long time and Jessica bent down to play with Harry. 'I'm sorry,' the attendant said eventually, 'this passport is nearly two years out of date.' Whose? How? That can't be right.

But Jessica had been so good at sorting out Harry's passport, along with everything else, that she hadn't noticed that her own had expired some months after our honeymoon. These were post 9/11 days, sure, but travel within Europe was supposed to be easy, so I couldn't imagine it would be a major issue. We both had our driving licences with us as we'd be driving a hire car, and I begged the girl to ask if a second form of ID would help. She did ring an office somewhere but the answer was unequivocal. I had visions of us having to drive to the passport office in Newport and queue for hours, before trying to get standby seats on a flight a couple of days later. But the advice we were given was different – and, in many ways, even less appealing.

'You and your son should fly today, with all your luggage,' explained the attendant. 'Your wife can get a new passport in Victoria and should be able to get on a flight tomorrow morning.' She might as well have told Jessica – whose face was crumpled as she fought back tears – to run to the moon. And I was terrified. I'd never had Harry alone for more than a couple of hours, let alone flown with him across Europe to a place I didn't know. And Jessica and I had barely been separated from each other for that long in the last five years.

Jessica unpacked her toothbrush and a change of clothes and put them, with her ticket, in her shoulder bag. After hugging and kissing both Harry and me, she headed for the train to Victoria, leaving one of her tears on my cheek. I talked it through with Harry, telling him it would be a boys' adventure and that we'd see Granny very soon and Mummy later. He didn't get it; and he didn't like it. 'Want Mummy. Where Mummy?' he cried repeatedly, as we made our way through the departure area.

We were browsing in Boots when Chris Routledge, co-owner of Coys and a friend, rang me. He'd had an email server crash at work and wanted me to come and fix it. 'I can't,' I told him. 'I'm about to get on a plane with Harry, and we've had to leave Jessica behind.'

'Bloody hell, that's a bummer,' he commiserated. Already a competent father of two, he clearly didn't much envy my position.

I thanked him for his sympathy, then guided him through a server reboot over the telephone.

'Good luck, mate,' said Chris, and Harry and I headed for the boarding gate.

For all my fears of a screaming, air-sick toddler, Harry was incredibly well behaved on the flight – so much so that the woman beside me commented on it. For his part, Harry bore the experience with stoicism, just reminding me periodically, 'See Mummy 'morrow.'

When we landed, it was late afternoon and very hot. I envied those passengers who had travelled in shorts. My jeans were hot and uncomfortable as I stood on the shuttle bus, clasping a wriggling Harry in my arms. He wanted to get down, but we were standing on the join of the bendy bus and the gaps in the concertina curtain wall looked too large to let him near, so he writhed and squirmed and I clung on, getting stickier and stickier. A couple of young teenaged girls watched us with amusement. Just you wait till you've got one, I thought.

I'd driven in Europe before, so driving on the wrong side of the road was OK, but I'd never driven a left-handed car before – a 'left hooker' as Jessica used to call them at work – and the cramped hire car was a challenge. The hand-drawn map I had on the back of an envelope was a mystery to the car-hire company manager, but she pointed me in the right direction for the address I gave her. Harry fell asleep in the back almost straight away, and I headed for the villa, wondering if I'd find it. Many times I went up and down various roads, passing the same roundabout three times, but finally, as much by luck as a process of elimination, I found what I was fairly sure was the right villa and unloaded our luggage onto the stone floor of the building.

It was soon dark, so I cooked the pasta that we had packed for Harry and left him to play with some toys – some of which we'd brought with us and others which came with the house.

As he played, I rang Jessica on her mobile. I was relieved to speak to her, but upset to hear the frustration and loneliness in her voice. She'd managed to get a new passport in a very short space of time, due partly – I have no doubt – to her Labrador eyes, as well as her very real tears and repeated insistence that she urgently needed to be with her baby. She was miserable – the budget hotel she was in was horrible and the pizza she'd ordered was cold and unappetising. Luckily though, she had managed to buy a new ticket on a late-morning flight, and as she blew us both kisses down the telephone, we willed the morning to come quickly.

When the late party arrived, my relief that Harry and I had planted ourselves in the right house and that we were no longer on our own was palpable. But it was nowhere near the sense of excitement and anticipation I felt as, the next morning, Christine, Harry and I drove back to the airport and waited outside the arrivals gate for Jessica.

We'd got there early, then learned that the flight was delayed, so we had hours to kill. We wandered around shops and sat looking at the papers. Harry ran round and round the banks of seats, climbing on them, then sliding on his tummy underneath them, and fluttering his eyelashes at pretty girls of all ages.

When Jessica's flight was announced, my heart leapt. I felt like a teenager, unable to hide my excitement. Then she came through, looking tired and stressed, and I ran to her calling, 'Harry, Harry, Mummy's here.' We hugged each other tightly and all of our conversation ran at a hundred miles an hour.

The week was a welcome sun-, sand- and water-filled break, with much exploration and plenty of wine and poolside barbecues in the evenings. It was also the one and only ever overseas family holiday for Harry, Jessica and me.

During one lazy, sun-soaked afternoon, Christine commented to Jessica and me, 'You know, I'd be so happy if my next grandchild was conceived on this holiday.'

Jessica was embarrassed. 'You can't say that, Mutts!' (Jessica often called her mum by this abbreviation of the German word for mother, *mutter*.) Little did Christine know how much Jessica and I wanted to conceive again, and how the fruitless last six months were not for lack of trying.

Day 3: Saturday, 26 June

In the morning Harry woke up, excited. 'Is Mummy here, Daddy?' he called.

Again, Jessica had to put the potentially unwelcome new member of the family quickly back in her Moses basket before I could let Harry in, so that he would not feel he had been usurped. Jessica's idea – she thought of everything. Harry ran around the bed, hugged his mother and looked over his shoulder at the strange little person beside her. He was naturally suspicious, but somehow realising she was here to stay, seemed to accept her as his baby sister almost immediately.

'Look what your baby sister has brought you, Harry,' I said to him, indicating a large box under a blanket next to my side of the bed.

My earliest identifiable memory is of my parents introducing me to my first sibling, Robert, when I was two years and four months old. I can recall the half-drawn curtains in their bedroom and a picnic rug barely covering a blue and white pedal tractor with a horn in the steering wheel. A packet of fruit pastilles was in the seat – the

46

best present my brother has ever given me! I wanted to recreate that moment for Harry.

After ten minutes of frenzied activity in his room as I hurriedly assembled his present for him, Harry proudly drove his yellow JCB tractor, complete with front scoop, into our bedroom, shrieking with delight.

'Look, Mummy, look! Look what my baby sister gived me!' We had no need to worry about sibling rivalry. Her offering had ensured that she was an instant success.

Jessica's temperature appeared to be down to normal in the morning, and the previous night's episode was forgotten in all the excitement. I prepared Jessica's breakfast of toast, cereal, yoghurt, decaf coffee and orange juice and delivered it to her in bed, then Harry and I had ours downstairs. She hardly ate anything, complaining of a sore throat, exacerbated by the toast. Concerned that I had clearly got the menu wrong, I nevertheless reminded her about keeping calories up for both energy and milk but didn't press the issue.

After a warm bath, Jessica looked in on the children's bedroom. 'Oh, it's gorgeous!' she said looking at the newly fitted carpet. We had already done so much to the house: we'd rewired, installed a new kitchen and decorated, as well as more recently replacing the 1970s blue bath, loo, basin and wall tiles in our bathroom with modern white ones and a terrific power shower. Harry had graduated from his cot-bed to a junior bed, well in advance of the new arrival so that he would not feel that anybody was 'stealing' his bed (another of Jessica's anti-jealousy ideas). Redecorating the children's bedroom had followed, and the carpet fitter had been in on Wednesday morning, so Jessica had barely had a chance to admire the room. Winnie the Pooh adorned the walls, both stickers and soft toys, and Jessica had bought matching curtains and a bean bag. It was all just as she had wanted it to be for the children. Our own room was still in a mess, but we would get round to that.

Then the whirlwind of family, flowers and messages of congratulation began. The first knock at the door was a delivery from a bakery in north London: a stunning basket of the most delicious cakes and biscuits sent by one of my clients. We were both touched, not only by the swiftness but also the thoughtfulness of this gesture. This was not the last time that they showed such amazing kindness.

That same morning we discussed names for our new baby. I was keen on Milly, but couldn't think of a name that could be shortened to this. Amelia? No, not a hit. Then a brainwave from Jessica – only one of her favourite names: Emily. Our daughter now had a first name and we agreed that she was to share Jessica's second – Kate. Emily Kate Palmer.

The telephone barely stopped ringing that day with me fielding the calls as Jessica wanted to rest. As I did so, I noticed that there was a message on our answering service from Karen, one of the midwives on St George's Hospital's Green Team, saying that Jessica was on her list, but that she was extremely busy that day and may not get to us. In light of the events of the previous evening I wasn't comfortable with this. I rang Karen back and explained about the shivers and high temperature. I asked whether she might, after all, make it over to us that day and she promised to put a mark next to Jessica's name and to make every effort. If not, she would definitely come the following day, Sunday. I queried the fever again, and she said that, should Jessica's temperature rise that evening (which she thought might be the case), I should give her a couple of Panadols. My concerns receded and I thanked her.

Mum came to visit on Saturday. Not wanting to be in the way or to sideline Harry, she didn't immediately go upstairs; instead she played with him in the sitting room, lavishing attention on him – her (chronologically) number-one grandchild.

After a while Harry told his Gran, 'I got a baby upstairs.'

'Have you?' Mum encouraged him.

'Yes, come and see!' You would have thought he had made her himself he was so proud.

So Mum went up with Harry and talked to Jessica for half an hour or so, before nervously asking, 'Does she have a name yet?' Jessica and I laughed as we'd totally forgotten to tell her that her first granddaughter was called Emily.

Mum had brought a huge chocolate cake for Harry, so that he felt a fuss was being made of him too. She told him it was a 'big brother cake'. That evening, however, he really played up and despite the fact that she was feeling well below par, Jessica hauled herself up and sat on the chair beside Harry's bed to read him a story.

Mum describes a lasting memory from that evening, just before she left, of Jessica propped up and gazing with total adoration at her new daughter lying on the bed beside her. She didn't move her head, just looked at Mum with a smile of joy and pride. There was in Jessica, Mum says, an absolute and beautiful serenity.

Day 4: Sunday, 27 June

After breakfast on Sunday I went on a mission. We hadn't dared to buy any new clothes without knowing whether Baby was a boy or girl. We had Harry's baby clothes, after all. But now that we knew, I was determined to go out and buy pink babygros. Anything would do, just so long as it was pink. I tried everywhere I could think of locally and failed miserably – all the shops were shut. I was disappointed, but Jessica was quite amused by my antics.

Laura and Jamie (her boyfriend) then Tim and Marian all arrived in the late morning. Jessica was just getting out of the bath when I went up to tell her she had visitors and I paused in the doorway to chat to her. She was dripping blood onto the bath mat and embarrassedly shooed me away.

'I don't mind; don't worry,' I told her – after all I'd seen far worse at the births of both of our children. But there was also the matter of a large, bright red area on her abdomen and while we weren't too alarmed by it, we were glad the midwife would be coming later.

Tim had brought some champagne – pink for a girl – which we opened while Jessica changed, then took it upstairs to toast mother and baby, both of whom were again lying on our bed. Jessica had a tiny sip, but soon put her glass down, saying that the bubbles hurt her sore throat. The house was full, noisy and very busy. Everyone was excited and although Jessica had been so looking forward to showing Emily off, the two of them remained upstairs in the bedroom.

At around midday, Karen, the community midwife arrived and I showed her upstairs.

'What are you doing in bed with a temperature, Jessica?' she asked as she walked in, seemingly surprised that a new mum should not yet be up and about, even though I had mentioned it to her on the phone.

The rest of us left them to it and went downstairs to the sitting room, where Harry entertained us. Karen stayed with Jessica for about three quarters of an hour or so, then came downstairs and we talked about her fever again. She thought the cause was probably a minor infection from before the delivery, as Jessica had complained of a sore gland in her neck on the previous Monday. She reiterated her instructions for taking Panadol and left some powder for us in an egg cup to sprinkle onto Emily's umbilicus, which wasn't as dry as it might have been.

When Karen left I went back up to see Jessica. I remember her laughing that Karen had been more interested in discussing contraception than anything else. Jessica said she had looked at her (no doubt with her twinkle in an eye) and asked, 'Do you think I'm interested in sex? That's what got me into this.' Jessica always had a quick, witty reply to everything.

Just before he left Jamie sneaked a look at both of the 'girls' lying on the bed. He, like Mum, talks about the serenity and look of pride and love in Jessica's face at that moment.

Later in the afternoon Christine came over and Jessica did briefly come downstairs, but the flurry of activity – a combination of baby, cooking Harry's supper and me fitting his buggy board to the back of the pram – proved too chaotic and stressful. Jessica retreated back upstairs.

Jessica always used to sing with Harry when he was in the bath. Sometimes she even got in with him, eliciting shrieks of delight and giggles. There would also be loud singing (from both of them), 'Five Speckled Frogs' being a particular favourite. I remember giving Harry a bath when he asked for the frog song and I had to admit to not knowing the words. But then Jessica came to the rescue, and started up from the bedroom opposite, much to Harry's delight. I can still hear them singing it together:

> Five little speckled frogs
> Sat on a speckled log
> Eating the most delicious bugs
> Yum! Yum!
>
> One jumped into the pool
> Where it was nice and cool
> Now there are four little speckled frogs.
> Glub! Glub!
>
> (Repeat with four, three, then two little speckled frogs . . .)
>
> One little speckled frog
> Sat on a speckled log
> Eating the most delicious bugs
> Yum! Yum!
>
> He jumped into the pool
> Where it was nice and cool

Now there are no more speckled frogs.
Glub! Glub!

Jessica allowed very few photographs to be taken of her after Emily was born. In the hospital I took a few of her feeding Emily, which I know will be treasured in years to come. Then, after we came home, I took some of Emily and Jessica took one of me together with the children, but she would not be photographed. 'My hair, look at me; I look awful,' she protested. Consequently, I believed the hospital photographs to be the last taken of her and the only ones of her with her precious daughter. Certainly, there was none of the four of us together.

It was only about four months later that I learned that Marian had taken a photograph of Jessica with Emily while she was resting in our bed, but hadn't dared to show it to me for ages. In it, Jessica is looking down at Emily, but, in hindsight, looks so ill. It was only a short time after the midwife had visited, yet she had missed this. Maybe we all had, thinking that she was just tired, and being reassured that the midwife had recommended nothing more than paracetamol.

```
From: Minette Palmer
To: Ben Palmer
Date: 27 June 2004 22:27
Subject: Baby Stuff


Hope all is well darling and Jessica is all
right, temperature & throat getting better?
It was lovely to get report from Laura and
Jamie but hope so many visitors weren't too
much for J?
Will be with you Tuesday about 12.30 with
lunch for all of you - meatballs (with gra-
vy), sliced potatoes baked in milk & a veg
```

(hope that's OK for Harry) + supper for Harry
(probably a pasta bake) + supper for you &
Jessica. IF it suits, I'll plan to leave between 5.30 and 5.45 that day.
Could you email me a list of anything you need
- I can get it en route from Tesco. So far
just have paper napkins!
Hope YOU are putting aside time to rest, relax
& have a snooze . . . zzz . . . zzzz . . .
quite often!
xxx Mum

Day 5: Monday, 28 June

From: Ben Palmer
To: Minette Palmer
Date: 28 June 2004 07:50
Subject: Baby Stuff

Thank you so much, that all sounds perfect.
Midwife very happy yesterday, but here for
ages with everyone downstairs - Jessica got
quite tired, but it couldn't be helped.
Throat better - soluble aspirin doing the
trick! Jessica has very sore hip/bottom
this a.m. (I think where Emily put pressure
on her during labour) - very uncomfortable
night. Trying to get midwife to come back
this a.m.; if not, Dr opens at 8, have to
drop notes off anyway so will try & get a
visit.

Lots of love,
Ben

From: Minette Palmer
To: Ben Palmer
Date: 28 June 2004 08:36
Subject: Baby Stuff

Very sorry to hear Jessica painful hip/bot-
tom. Best plan to get doctor to visit her.
xxx Mum

During Sunday night Jessica had been very uncomfortable with a pain in her hip and pelvis, so first thing on Monday morning she called our doctors' surgery and had a telephone consultation with one of the GPs – a Dr Williams – who told her she may have sciatica or could have slipped a disc. It seemed a bit strange, but it is suppos- edly not uncommon in late pregnancy and we accepted her opinion. I collected a prescription for Diclofenac (an anti-inflammatory pain- killer), dropped off Jessica's discharge letter from the hospital and picked up the tablets from the chemist's next to the surgery pretty much straight away.

From: Ben Palmer
To: Minette Palmer
Date: 28 June 2004 08:52
Subject: Baby Stuff

Jessica spoken to Dr at length. Slipped disc
in labour and must have now jarred it. Anti-
inflammatory painkillers on way. Harry happy
at prospect: he gets to try out the buggy
board!

From: Minette Palmer
To: Ben Palmer
Date: 28 June 2004 09:47
Subject: Baby Stuff

So glad it all sounds OK. Give J my love.
Keep an eye on her - if the pain feels like
sore pressure inside or you're worried, doctor
is there to be consulted!
[It is possible to get a haematoma after a
birth; a friend had one after one of her
babies. No one believed her until it burst
with a whoosh. Don't tell J about this as it
sounds a bit scary - it's something for you
just to be aware of.]
xxx Mum

From: Catherine Donner
To: Ben Palmer
Date: 28 June 2004 11:34
Subject: Baby Stuff

Darling Ben, Jessica & Harry,
WELCOME TO EMILY - CONGRATULATIONS
I am so thrilled to hear the news and that
Emily is huge and well. You must be so excited
and I hope Harry likes his little sister.
Sorry about the impersonal email, but somehow
a baby card hasn't materialised . . . Also,
I had a look in my suitcase of wool and found
nothing in pink - except a hand-wash item
which I am sure you don't want and which, in
any case, would probably be too small.

Can I come and baby worship when life has settled down? Let me know (preferably by phone
as the email isn't working quite right).
Am sorry to hear Jessica has had some problems. Take lots of care - all of you.
Love to everyone and I hope to come and
meet Emily very soon (and perhaps have a
cuddle?).
Much love,
Catherine XXXX

From: Irena Brewis
To: Ben Palmer
Date: 28 June 2004 13:05
Subject: Congratulations!!

My dears,
How fabulous to hear of the birth of your
daughter. Congratulations! We are thrilled
for you and glad to know that Jessica and babe
are well.
With fondest love,
Irena

At just after three o'clock in the afternoon I ran into Jess, one of our
neighbours, who was on her way to the park with another mum and
all their children. I told her that Jessica was in bed with a slipped
disc, so she popped up to see her. Jessica was feeding Emily and
watching the tennis on TV. She was hot and sweaty, complaining
at how unfair it was that she was stuck in bed. Jess only stayed for
five or ten minutes; she said she thought Jessica's speech was a
little slurred, but put it down to the Diclofenac.

Another neighbour, Donna, also dropped by and very sweetly

brought a plant, but I didn't push her to come in for fear of things getting too busy and overloading Jessica as had been the case the day before.

I, like Jessica, was annoyed that she was still in bed, and she wasn't in the best of moods either. My irritation was exacerbated when, as I stood in our bedroom window looking down onto the street, I saw a neighbour with her first baby, born earlier the same day as Emily and in the same hospital, getting into her car and driving off. It just didn't seem fair.

From: Ben Palmer
To: Vanessa Marcais
Date: 28 June 2004 20:17
Subject: Baby Girl!

Ness,
I'm sorry to be so crap about letting you know
(but you know what it's like!) - Jess had
a relatively short & uncomplicated labour &
gave birth to Emily on Thursday at 6.26 p.m.
weighing a mere 9lb 13oz!
She's had a fairly rough time since, though,
with temperatures & a slipped disc, but is
well on the way; & baby is doing very well,
and demands food with menaces! Harry is a very
proud big brother (and also the proud owner of
a brand new pedal tractor with working bucket!
Well done, Emily, how did you know?).
Do give her a ring soon, and we'd love to see
you before you go back to Paris.
Lots of love,
Ben, Jess, Harry & Emily xxx

One of Jessica's NCT friends, Nicola, telephoned during the day with congratulations and asked if she could come round. But again, worried about another exhausting day for Jessica, we arranged for her to visit on Wednesday instead.

Meanwhile, the drugs Jessica had been prescribed seemed to be doing their job and the rest of Monday passed without incident in a cycle of baby feeds and short naps.

Day 6: Tuesday, 29 June

From: Vanessa Marcais
To: Ben Palmer
Date: 29 June 2004 08:00
Subject: Baby Girl!

Welcome to the world, Emily, wonderful news.
Love and kisses,
Ness, Flavien and Oliver xxx

Jessica had had an extremely uncomfortable night and was unable to sit up in the morning to feed Emily.

'Why didn't you wake me in the night instead of suffering alone?' I asked her and gave Emily her first formula-only feed.

Jessica really was in a lot of pain at this point, but I was unkind and short tempered with her. How can you spoil our happiness with complaints of being sore? I wondered. Of course you're sore: you've just delivered an oversized baby. I could kick myself now for having had those thoughts, albeit fleeting.

As I was getting Harry ready for school, I looked in on her again and added, 'If it's still that bad, call the bloody doctor again.'

'What do you bloody think I'm bloody doing?' she answered, holding the telephone to her ear.

I slunk away and took Harry to nursery school.

I was standing in line at the cash machine, waiting to get some money out in order to run some errands for Jessica when my mobile rang. Jessica said urgently, 'The doctor can see me right now. Where are you? Can you come home? We have to be there before ten.' I left the queue and hurriedly drove home.

When I got home Jessica was dressed and downstairs, waiting with Emily. I bundled them both into the car and drove to the surgery around the corner in the next street up from ours. I helped Jessica into the surgery and we were sent straight in to see the doctor. She was suffering from lower-back pain and what she described as stiffness or cramps in her right arm and leg and walking was an enormous effort. They were swollen, which the doctor didn't like any more than Jessica did. After speaking to a registrar at Kingston she said she would call an ambulance to our house 'on blues' in six minutes to give us a chance to get home. She was being sent to Thameside, a different maternity ward at the hospital. I took Jessica, Emily and the referral letter home and packed a bag with a few things for her hopefully short stay back at Kingston.

While I ran up and down the stairs Jessica sat quietly on the sofa, looking tired and weak; she sat in the same place where we'd always sat, watching television, reading, talking and laughing. In the evenings after supper, Jessica would often put her legs up on mine. She always asked if I minded. She knew I always loved her to, but would never assume anything.

While we were waiting for the ambulance I called Mum, who was due to come up again to help later that day. I told her I was taking Jessica back to hospital and asked if she could collect Harry from school at lunchtime. I said I would leave his car seat in the hall and the house keys with a neighbour. She promised to leave immediately – with her toothbrush. Then I posted the keys through Jess' door, in an envelope marked: 'Jessica gone to hospital. Mum will pick up keys.'

The ambulance seemed to be taking an age – certainly longer than the six minutes we'd been promised. I rang the surgery to check on it and they told me that this was normal – it could take up to an hour. On blues? Surely not. I could easily have got Jessica to the hospital myself by now, albeit probably in less comfort.

Almost an hour after we'd seen the doctor I had a call from Ambulance Control. The woman on the phone apologised profusely and explained that they'd been given the address of a pregnant mother in Wimbledon who had, apparently, been in the surgery at the same time as us. While she was confirming our address, I heard the scream of a siren coming down the street. An ambulance pulled up outside our house and I went outside to meet it.

Jessica was by now very grey, very quiet, listless and short of breath. The two paramedics gave her oxygen, moved her to the ambulance in a chair and started to prepare her for the journey back to Kingston General.

I loaded Emily, now five days old, into her car seat and strapped it into the car. With my heart pounding, I put my head round the ambulance door and told Jessica, 'Don't worry, you'll be fine. I'll see you soon.' I really wanted to believe it, but was beginning to feel very, very uncertain. Then I set off ahead of the ambulance, thinking of Harry who would be so excited when I told him that Mummy had been in an ambulance, but equally cross that he'd missed it!

I talked to Emily as I drove to keep myself calm and had got as far as Putney Vale before I saw the ambulance in my rear-view mirror. 'Get out of the bloody way, that's my wife,' I yelled at a driver 300 metres behind me who wouldn't pull over. Seconds later, the ambulance passed me and at that point I felt a rush of panic and anxiety. 'Don't leave me behind, Percy,' I said out loud. I wanted to put my foot down and chase the ambulance, but resisted the temptation.

As I reached the hospital car park an ambulance pulled out and turned into the Accident & Emergency gate, but I thought nothing of it as I parked the car and carried Emily, still in her car seat, up to the maternity suite where I had been told Jessica would be taken.

'No, she's not here; she's gone to Worcester,' a helpful receptionist announced to me after consulting her records. Worcester was the ward that Jessica and Emily had been moved to the previous Thursday evening, once the porter had eventually materialised after the Euro 2004 England–Portugal game. I set off, relieved that the problem was minor enough for her to be back there again.

But in Worcester I was greeted with 'Jessica who?' Looking back, their confusion was understandable. Jessica and Emily had been discharged four days earlier, so what was this madman doing there now with his baby, looking for his wife? A short telephone call revealed that Jessica was in A&E.

What? Shit, it's really not meant to be that bad. My heart racing, I flew back across the car park, Emily swinging in her seat.

I saw an ambulance outside A & E and the driver, recognising me, opened her door and said, 'Don't worry; her blood pressure dropped as we arrived, so we redirected. It's routine. She'll be fine.'

Ok, I told myself. Relax. I now realised that this had to have been the ambulance I'd seen earlier.

I checked in at A & E reception and was immediately shown through from the casualty waiting area to the blue family room. Hell, special treatment already. A nurse went in search of a sterile bottle with which to feed Emily. Ready-mixed cartons of formula – a lifesaver for the parent in a hurry.

Eventually a doctor came and spoke to me. I don't remember now who he was but we had met briefly in the delivery room the week before. I suppose he must have been a consultant gynaecologist. He told me that the swelling in Jessica's arm and leg could be due to blood clots, but that the physicians – he described them as 'the really clever doctors' – would be doing blood tests and would explain everything.

After a long wait another, younger, doctor came in. Jessica did not have a pulmonary clot so they weren't overly concerned if there were any anywhere else. They did, however, suspect an infection. They were stabilising her blood pressure and she was becoming more comfortable. He said that someone from Critical Care (the High-dependency and Intensive-care Units) would be coming to see her; 'They have some really clever drugs over there for these sorts of things,' he told me. It just gets better and better, I thought. Where is my wife and why does she need all these clever things? I wondered. I was on the verge of panic, but everyone else seemed calm and confident, so I tried to draw strength and comfort from this.

I waited in that blue room for what seemed like an eternity. I followed the pattern in the carpet with my eyes, tracing it around the room. I fed Emily. I rocked her. I paced up and down with her then put her in her car seat to sleep, but she barely managed to. Every once in a while someone looked in on me.

'Are you with the lady in there?" The woman indicated the resuscitation room behind her with a tilt of her head.

I nodded.

'I'm sure they'll let you go and see her soon.' I desperately wanted to go straight in and see her then – I was getting so anxious – but they were 'working on her' I was told.

Eventually another doctor, the 'physician', came into the family room. It transpired that Jessica did indeed have an infection. And septicaemia. She would be moved at some point to the High Dependency Unit where she would be for three or four days, I was told.

Oh my God. This means I've got to look after two children, on my own, until then. And I bet they'll keep her in a ward for a week afterwards. Do they have any idea how difficult that's going to be?

A student paediatric nurse was found to look after Emily for me while I went outside to use my mobile. Finding myself next to an ashtray I remember thinking at that point how much I wished I was still a smoker. I got through to Christine first.

'Christ, Ben. Septicaemia? That's really serious.' Tell me about it, I thought. I filled her in as much as I could, reassured her and said I would call again if there was more news. She promised to tell Tim for me. I think I must also have called Mum at our house as well, although I don't actually remember.

Once back inside the hospital, I asked if I could go in and see Jessica; they weren't entirely happy as the paediatric nurse had vanished and resus' is no place for a healthy newborn baby. After a long wait and a discussion with the doctor though, we were shown in 'for a few minutes' as they were quiet.

I was so relieved. Jessica was propped up, some colour back in her cheeks and smiling at us both.

'It's not my fault; it's nothing to do with not taking my tablets,' she told me, defiantly. When Jessica had first complained of cramps in the early hours of that morning, I had been irritated at my loss of sleep and asked her if she was still taking her assorted pregnancy vitamins and supplements. When she said she had forgotten to, I had tutted, as if to say 'I told you so' and rolled over. What a bastard I'd been.

'Of course it's not, Perc,' I told her. 'You're going to be fine – they'll look after you now.'

She looked at me with her big brown eyes, and said, 'I'm really sorry – I'm on warfarin. I can't breast feed Emily.' We both believed in 'Breast is Best' and Jessica had fed Harry herself for six months. She felt she was letting us all down.

'It doesn't matter Percy. You can express your milk until you're better. You'll have to throw it away, but Emily will be fine on formula for a week or so.'

Jessica did look so much better now – indeed beautiful, radiating love and affection. She was concerned about Harry's lunch and wanted to know who had picked him up from school. I explained and reassured her – Mum had been coming up for the day anyway, so she was managing things at home to perfection.

Just then Jessica saw a doctor walk past and called out, 'Where are my drugs?' She was ordering morphine like it was wine and the doctor a waiter. That's my girl, Percy, I thought. You make them look after you! Still, I just couldn't believe how much better she looked already. These truly were amazing doctors! Of course, she was being given morphine so she was high as a kite and being pumped with goodness knows what else to keep her blood pressure up. Artificially.

Jessica sent me home with Emily and I promised to return later, once she was settled. It was no place for a baby, and there'd be a long wait until she was moved to HDU; it made sense.

How I wish now that I had stayed and talked. But there was no way we could have known then what the next 22 hours had in store. Regret – so easy, yet so pointless. I really thought things would be all right. Everybody did.

On the drive home a client friend rang me. I am fortunate in that a lot of my clients are friends and some of my friends are clients. Many moons ago Jessica had also worked for Chris and I told him what was happening. I think my fear must have come across, but he reassured me, saying that HDU was a fancy name for being watched a bit more closely. His wife is a nurse practitioner, so he must know, I thought. I didn't really believe him, but maybe I was overly worried. I can do that quite well.

At home I helped Mum to get Harry and Emily into a routine and made sure they were all right. Harry had missed the excitement of the ambulance and was asking me where Mummy was. I didn't hide anything, but told him in the best way I could for a three year old that Mummy had got a sore tummy and that an ambulance had taken her to hospital so the doctors could make her better. He accepted my word. Why shouldn't he have? If Daddy said everything was OK then it must be; grown-ups just know these things.

When I got back to Kingston General it must have been around half past six. I found Critical Care, was buzzed in through the main door and then rang through from the waiting room. I was told to come straight down the corridor. Jessica was in an Intensive Care bed. She was surrounded by machines and a tree of drips were being fed into her. She did not look at all well. Her breathing was difficult and she was extremely weak. This was not what I had expected after the last time I had seen her. I was quite alarmed, but tried not to show it.

Jessica smiled when she saw me and tried to sit up. The alarms went off and she fell back down again. She was confused, but wanted to know that everything was all right at home. Good, I thought – you've got the machine that goes 'ping'; I recalled a Monty Python sketch involving a woman in labour and a lot of expensive equipment. Once she had settled back down she asked for a drink of water which she drank awkwardly through a straw. Then she said she wanted to go for a walk. I was taken aback – this was obviously not going to happen. I was unnerved by her asking for what she so clearly couldn't have, and didn't want to be the one to tell her she couldn't have it. I told her we'd ask the sister when she came back and in the meantime we settled for conversation.

Jessica told me in some detail what was happening to her: her kidneys had ceased to function and her liver wasn't working properly. I couldn't believe what I was hearing, neither could I believe just how calm she appeared. On her return to Jessica's station a sister then explained further to me what the position was: the infection and septicaemia were being fought with antibiotics which were being continually pumped into her body via an automated syringe. They were also giving her more powerful drugs to keep her blood pressure up.

The sister explained about the kidney failure and about how when the body is under attack from a toxic infection and is short of oxygen, the organs shut down in order of least importance, starting with the kidneys. I was told that they might need to put Jessica on dialysis in the morning. (I have since heard a statistic that there is an 85–90 per cent mortality rate in patients in ICU who go onto dialysis. How scary is that? Thank God I didn't know that then.) My poor, poor Percy. What was happening to her?

The staff seemed to be optimistic, although the sister did say that they would normally have hoped for a better response by now. When I turned back to Jessica, she looked at me and asked, 'You do understand, don't you?' I said I did and she smiled and relaxed.

Did she know more than the rest of us, I have often asked myself. I doubt it. Yet she did show enormous wisdom and calm.

I had brought in a small, folding photograph wallet that Jessica took everywhere with her. In it were two pictures of me from before we were married, but I had inserted a passport photograph of Harry over one of mine before I took it to her at the hospital. It had been with her in the hospital when both Harry and Emily were born and had gone on holidays with her. I hadn't remembered to pack it in her bag that morning and somehow that didn't seem right. I asked if it could be put up, but there are no bedside tables in ICU. It was put on a shelf at the back of the cubicle, but not where Jessica could see it. It would have to do for now though.

I was given Jessica's watch and jewellery in a brown envelope. Don't they usually do that when someone has died? The alarm must have shown in my face, as it was explained to me that jewellery interferes with x-rays and treatment and that they don't have anywhere to store valuables. It was normal, nothing sinister. Another sister who had returned to Jessica's station then gave me back the unnecessary clobber I had sent her in with, including the box of Diclofenac, saying we might as well keep it for another time. Didn't Percy need it? I was so confused. She also said I might want to bring some make-up and scent next time I came in. It would make Jessica feel more human among all the science and technology, I supposed.

Then they explained how Intensive Care worked – how I was welcome to be there at any time of day or night, but that I might find it easier to visit during regular afternoon visiting hours, as I would be asked to sit in the family room when Jessica was being seen by a consultant or if they were treating her.

Jessica was so weak. She drifted in and out of consciousness as talking used up her oxygen levels, the monitors bleeping every time her oxygen fell. I was alarmed at first, but then it was explained to me and I would watch as her saturation levels fell, then she'd go silent and close her eyes. Slowly the level of oxygen in her blood would rise again and Jessica would open her eyes and continue talking as though there had been no break in our conversation. It was heartbreaking to be so close to her yet unable to do something – unable to make a difference.

I could see that my being there wasn't helping and Jessica obviously needed rest. I promised to come back the next afternoon during regular visiting hours. Then I stroked her arm, kissed her and said goodbye.

If only I had known it was for ever.

There are so many things you want to say when it's too late. I could have stayed while she slept. I could have stayed all night. I didn't know I needed to. All I knew was that our children needed me and I needed sleep.

But Jessica needed me more. Why didn't she ask? I'd have stayed.

I was so scared as I drove home. I couldn't believe this nightmare. What had happened to leave her lying there so weak in an intensive care bed, surrounded by machinery?

I was stuck in a traffic jam on the road down the hill into South-fields when a client – Fiona from Hurlingham School, who had sent the cakes – called to remind me about a printer I needed to buy. All I could manage, tears falling as I spoke, was, 'Fi, she's really, really ill.' Immediately, the printer lost all importance for Fiona and she told me not to even think about work until Jessica was better. She was so kind and understanding but I just kept thinking, No, you need that printer, I'll sort it out. And anyway, I told her, I couldn't afford not to work. It took me about three months, but I did get them their printer in the end.

I stood in the kitchen after supper that evening while Mum cleared up. I was gripping the edge of the work surface with both hands. 'She can't leave me, Mum. She can't leave me,' I said.

Shocked and surprised, Mum comforted me, saying that Jessica was in the best possible place and that she was sure she would be all right. She hadn't seen what I had seen, though, and although I didn't think – or couldn't believe – the worst would happen, I had been shaken by my visit to ICU. I was terrified. Events were spiral-ling out of control.

From: Robert Palmer
To: Ben Palmer
Date: 29 June 2004 09:50
Subject: <no subject>

Dear Ben,
Just a very short note to let you know that we are both thinking of Jessica and all of you so much, and send every possible good wish and prayer. Please do pass them on to Jessica too.
I won't add to your burden by calling - but please do feel free to be in touch if there's anything either of us can do to help - shopping, babysitting, whatever. Katherine is off work now and is available any time as well.
Much love to you both,
Robert and Katherine

From: Ben Palmer
To: Robert Palmer
Date: 29 June 2004 22:53
Subject: Re: <no subject>

Thank you, very much. It means a lot that so many people are thinking of her. I'm sure she'll be all right, but right now she needs all the help she can get.
Love to you both,
Ben

Already feeling as though I was living in a parallel world, I went to bed after supper, but lay awake, weighing everything up in my head.

It was all so frightening and unknown. I was scared, but knew that Jessica was safe. She was, as I had told her, in the best possible place and in the best possible hands. My world had been turned upside down though. I was juggling concern for my wife with looking after Harry and the needs of a newborn baby who now had to be bottle-fed. I didn't know where to be or what to think, but I knew that at the moment the children needed me to be with them. Others were looking after Jessica, and she herself wanted to know that I was coping with the children's needs. Eventually I fell asleep, a jumble of confused thoughts spinning around in my head.

Day 7:
Wednesday, 30 June

At half past one in the morning the telephone rang, but by the time I'd identified the new and quieter ring in our bedroom (intended not to disturb Jessica during the day if she was asleep) as the telephone, the caller had rung off. Who would ring in the middle of the night? I panicked. Called 1471. Number withheld. What to do? But three minutes later Christine rang. The hospital had tried her next. Thank goodness I had given the hospital her details as well as my own, even though they had said it wasn't necessary. Jessica's condition had deteriorated and she had had to be sedated and put onto a ventilator. We both said we would get there as soon as we could.

I didn't register the severity of the situation, although looking back it was obvious. I dressed. I undressed. I waited until 2 a.m. when I fed Emily, then dressed again. I knocked on the sitting-room door to try and wake Mum who was asleep on a makeshift camp bed in there, as we had no spare room. No response. I knocked louder. Nothing. I went in and turned on the overhead lights. She had earplugs in! I woke her up, explained what was happening and left her in charge.

I drove back to the hospital on empty roads, totally confused. I was led straight through to Jessica's bedside. Oh my God! Sheer horror. She was unconscious, under anaesthesia, bright red in the face due to a searing temperature, but also under a thermal blanket to try and keep her skin temperature up. She had already been put on dialysis, and her chest rose and fell in time with the ventilator. So small and so helpless and her hand so cold as I held it.

It was then and only then that the sisters let on that they were worried.

'Is she going to die?' I asked at one point, although I didn't really want to hear the answer.

'She may do, yes,' they said.

This wasn't right. It wasn't meant to happen like this. She's a mother, I thought. She's got a brand new baby. We're meant to be happy for God's sake. Our whole lives are ahead of us. There I was, standing at my darling wife's bedside, watching as she fought for her life. There was nothing I could do. I have never felt so useless. In the eleven and a half years I knew Jessica she only ever really asked one thing of me.

'Protect me. Look after me, won't you?' she had asked. Surely I could have done that now? Made everything all right again? Fight, damn you. Fight for your life.

They had doubled medication dosages and were trying risky, last-resort drugs. They doubled the dose again and still the infection raged. They had x-rayed, scanned and tested but just didn't know where the primary source of the infection was.

Christine and I sat or stood beside Jessica's bed and waited. At one point someone changed the collection tank on the dialysis machine. I had never seen so much urine. 'That's one big pee,' I joked. Nobody else thought it was funny. It wasn't. This was life or death.

From time to time we were sent back to the family room while the medical staff carried out 'procedures'. We spent hours in that room. We drank tea and we talked. We ran over the same conversations again and again. Eventually we just sat in silence.

I stared out at the yellow street lights in the dark night sky and watched the dawn rise. I saw nurses and hospital workers arriving for work. I paced up and down the dimly lit corridors, just for a change of scene. Just for something to do. On one such walk along the corridor from the family room to Jessica's bed I caught sight of the alcohol hand-rub dispenser on the wall, with its message about cleanliness. I pushed down on the pump and rubbed the gel over my hands. We didn't want to take any germs in with us, after all.

So many people knew what was happening by now – family, friends and clients alike. There was enormous support and I knew many, many people were praying for us. But nobody was really expecting what was to come.

I know that around this time, Mum spoke to Laura and told her, 'I think Ben's really frightened he's going to lose his wife.' Laura told me her reaction – despite her medical knowledge and experience – was, 'No. No, that just isn't going to happen. It can't.'

Who would have imagined it? That sort of thing happens in films. To other people. Never you. Possibly not even someone you know.

I became anxious that we had been waiting for so long. I started pacing again, reading notices and looking at the staff photograph board, counting the many faces I recognised. One of the sisters I had spoken to, but who was now looking after another patient, saw me there and went to check at Jessica's station as to whether we could go back in. We were allowed to see Jessica, but there was no change.

Harry's wake-up and breakfast time were now fast approaching. I desperately wanted to be at home when he woke up as just a day earlier we had both felt that keeping him in a familiar routine was the most important thing. So I kissed Jessica and promised the sister I would return again in the afternoon, reverting to my original plan of coming in during visiting hours.

I drove home in tears and managed to crawl into bed and grab forty minutes sleep before Harry woke up, just after seven o'clock. I was totally exhausted and felt almost robot-like as I tried to be in two places at once, being very concerned about Jessica but also struggling, even with Mum's support, to look after our young son and newborn baby.

At half past seven the telephone rang. It was a sister calling from the ICU. I didn't recognise her name or her voice so the shift must have changed again.

'What plans have you got to come in today?' she asked.

'I'll come in after two,' I said. 'I was told it was easier.'

'You might want to come in earlier.' That was a statement, not a question, as I had heard it.

'I don't want to be in the way or to have to spend the morning in the waiting room.' (The mornings are the busiest time in ICU, I was learning, and you can be removed from the bedside regularly.)

Listen to what she's telling you, I urged myself. You're not listening.

'On Jessica's chart it says she's non-practising Church of England.'

'Well, yes . . .' Non-practising was a bit strong; we do try and go to church sometimes, mainly to Blackmoor when staying with my parents at Burhunt, as Harry was christened there and the vicar, April, is a wonderful, kind lady. My thoughts were drifting from the conversation. I wasn't awake enough to focus on what was being said to me.

'Would you like us to call a chaplain from any particular faith?'

'Oh Christ. I know what you're saying. I'll be there straight away.' No, no, no.

I had obviously been aware that Jessica was ill, but had, I think, been blanking out the true extent. Partly, this was because the staff had all seemed so calm and confident, talking about 'when she's moved out of ICU', but it must also have been a denial of my worst fears. Now the penny had dropped. The pretence of normality that I was holding onto was shattered and my world started to crumble and fall away.

I jumped in and out of the shower to wake myself up properly, explained to Mum about the phone call and drove like a maniac. Just try and stop me, officer, I thought. I don't care any more.

I reached the hospital at around ten past eight. Christine had also just arrived and a doctor was outlining the position. It was not at all good. The treatment wasn't working. They had done all they could do. They couldn't increase the doses and there was nothing stronger. Even with the dialysis filtering out toxins, the levels were rising in her blood.

Shaking, I went through to see Jessica. Her face was blue and cold, like the rest of her body had been in the night. She was cold, clammy and stiff. This isn't my wife, I thought. Where is she? I could not believe what I was seeing. The pain and distraction of seeing her was immense.

All I could think was, Perc, this isn't right. You can pull through. We haven't finished yet; there's still so much to do. Everything around me was becoming a blur. I just didn't understand. This isn't my life, I told myself. I've obviously fallen into somebody else's. It's a dream. A nightmare. Somebody wake me up.

Jessica had been fine. Harry's labour and delivery had been far longer and harder than Emily's. Nothing went wrong then. What the hell was happening now?

Christine and I went back to the waiting room for quite some time. The midwife who had delivered Emily came in and sat with us. She had heard what was happening when she'd arrived for her shift and had come straight over from Maternity. She was in tears. We hugged. She sweetly said that she thought she must be intruding, but I asked her to stay for as long as she could. It was helpful for me to have somebody there from the hospital who I felt knew Jessica and me, even just a little.

A succession of doctors, clinical directors, anaesthetists and surgeons came in and out to talk to us and try and explain the situation. Very little sunk in at the time. The consultant gynaecologist talked to me at length. She said that they had done everything they could with one exception. They could open Jessica up in theatre and try to remove the infected area in her abdomen. (They could only guess that it was either part of her gut or her womb.) My immediate reaction was that they shouldn't operate. Jessica had been terrified of having a Caesarean and it was by now obvious to us all that she was going to die. I told the consultant that I didn't want Jessica butchered. She didn't take offence.

Amidst all of this, we were wondering where Tim was. Nobody had been able to get hold of him. He had to be told, he had to be involved, but time was running out. Eventually, he called the hospital back and someone spoke to him. 'I'm on my way,' was all he said.

With a million thoughts running round my head, suddenly it dawned on me that there would be a post-mortem, so what difference would surgery make? And, as it was pointed out to me, at least Harry and Emily could then be told that there really was nothing else that could have been done. That clinched it and I gave the surgeon permission to operate.

Because of the dialysis, Jessica's blood had been thinned too much for surgery – she would have just bled to death – so she had to be given Factor VIII over the next hour to enable her blood to coagulate. We waited and talked and waited some more. The agony of waiting was unbearable. Tears fell as I struggled to comprehend the horror that was surrounding us. The hospital chaplain on duty, Father Grant, came and sat and talked as well. But nothing that anyone said could make any sense of it all.

I asked the consultant whether any member of Jessica's – by now – extensive team thought she had any chance of surviving both the surgery and the remaining septicaemia even if the primary infection was removed. She shook her head. I think they wanted to operate so that we would all know that everything conceivable had been done. And perhaps there was always a chance in a billion. But ultimately, while I didn't want to believe her, I knew she was right.

I wanted to scream and shout. Where had it gone wrong? Why Jessica? Why me? Why any of us?

When they were nearly ready to operate, we went through to ICU and I stood near Jessica. The place was a hive of activity and preparation. There must have been twenty or more people milling around. I couldn't get close enough to Jessica to touch her, so I asked someone to move the machinery so that I could stand at the end of the bed. Then I crawled under tubes and across wires and stood behind her and held her head. I kissed her and talked to her, saying the same things again and again. A tear dropped onto her forehead and I brushed it away with my cheek.

'Don't leave me, Perc, please don't leave me. I love you, for Christ's sake. You can't leave me.' As if she wanted to. I don't even know if she was still there, she was connected to so many machines. Had they turned them off she would probably have died there and then.

Eventually, when they were ready to move Jessica the short distance into theatre, I kissed her again and said goodbye and we watched her being wheeled out. I had to sit down. Luckily, someone second-guessed me, and caught me in a chair.

After staring for a moment at the empty space where the bed had been, we went back to the waiting room – Christine, Father Grant, the midwife and I.

I prayed for a miracle; we needed one – of biblical proportions. We waited.

But not for long enough. Within half an hour or so the consultant was back in the room. I knew. Not enough time.

She just said, 'I'm so sorry.'

Blackness. Dizziness. I cried out. The world around me shut down in a white fog. I was on my own. I was shaking. I felt sick.

They had opened Jessica's abdomen and she had arrested. She just couldn't cope with any more. My brave, brave Percy just couldn't fight any longer. Her heart had stopped at 11.20 a.m. Three cycles of CPR were performed, but to no avail. They stitched her up again, without even finding the primary infection. I was told that all of her insides looked as her skin had done beforehand. Blue with cyanosis. Jessica's death was officially recorded at 11.50 a.m.

How could this happen? How could God have let it happen? I had begged Him again and again over the last few hours to help her, to intervene, but He hadn't listened. The one time in her life she had really needed Him, it hadn't done any good. I would have sold my soul to Him or the Devil if either had offered me her life, but there was no one there for her. What sort of a world is this? Why take a brilliant mother when there were so many bad ones? There weren't any reasons. There weren't any answers. It was all so pointless.

My mobile rang. Hell, it shouldn't be on in here. But nobody seemed to mind. The number displayed was Sally's, Chris' wife. I couldn't speak. I had to switch the phone off. Percy was dead. That was it. Nothing mattered. The end of our beautiful world. Our invincibility had been smashed.

Everyone said all the right things and slipped away, back to their duties. Then, after what felt like an eternity we were told that Jessica had been moved to a room just along the corridor and that we could go and see her. Christine kindly said I should go alone and that she would follow on. I was shown into a semi-darkened room and the door was closed. Percy looked so calm and peaceful, lying in a pristine bed in a perfectly white gown, but she looked so cold. All of the lines and tubes were gone, except for the main ventilator tube which, tied in place with a bandage, had bruised the side of her mouth. I understand it has to be left in place until after any post mortem.

I collapsed beside her and held one of her hands between my own. Her arm was so blue, so cold and stiff and so unbelievably heavy. I kissed her again and again and cried into the sleeve of her gown. What was I going to do? Who was I now? I talked and talked to her, though for the life of me I can't now remember what I said. It probably didn't even make sense. Someone had placed her photographs next to her. I put them in my pocket to bring home and return to their place on her bedside table, beside her half-reread and much-thumbed copy of *Frenchman's Creek* with her favourite bookmark stuffed into it.

In the end, when I could stand the silence in the room no longer, I went to find Christine. Father Grant offered to perform the Last Rites. Christine was, I think, against the idea, but I asked him to do it anyway. Despite my religious doubts, I believe in getting all the help one can. We went and stood beside Jessica. Father Grant gave her the Last Rites beautifully, anointing her palms and lips with oil and saying, 'Your sins are forgiven.' What sins? I wondered. Jessica never hurt anyone. She was a good and kind person.

Afterwards, Christine said to me simply, 'Thank you. I'm glad you asked him to do that.'

Tim had still not arrived at the hospital, but by this point I had to get out. I was choking from claustrophobia and I desperately wanted to see our children. My children. Christine said she'd stay and wait for him.

The corridor was bustling with porters, patients, nurses and visitors carrying flowers, no doubt looking forward to seeing their loved ones. Halfway along I saw Tim walking towards me at speed, but with that characteristic gait. Christ, what would I say? How could I tell him? We drew closer and closer to one another. It seemed to take an eternity, like slow motion.

'How is she?' Tim asked.

I started crying. 'Tim, she's dead.'

How many times would I say that? I still do. 'She's dead.' What else can you say? There's nothing easy about Jessica's death; how can I try and find an easy way to say it? She didn't 'pass away' – that suggests going peacefully, in one's sleep and at a ripe old age. I certainly didn't 'lose' her – that would imply carelessness on my part. She had just been torn, brutally, from us.

Tim's face registered utter disbelief. I took him back to the waiting room to Christine and left them again.

All these people in the corridor passing me; didn't they care? But how could they possibly know? Still, I felt so angry.

I drove home feeling numb and isolated. Tears clouded my eyes and I struggled to keep them at bay so I could see the road. I let myself into the house and found Mum with Emily. She had just started to give her a bottle. Harry was at a neighbour for the afternoon, playing. I stood in the sitting-room doorway and looked at them both.

'She didn't make it, Mum.' Poor Mum was devastated and wanted to hug me and I desperately needed one but she couldn't until Emily had finished feeding.

A short while later I was sitting on my bed running my hands through my hair, saying, 'She's dead; Jessica's dead,' over and over, as though repeating it would somehow help me to understand it, when Mum's mobile rang. I answered it. I didn't stop to think.

It was my sister-in-law, Katherine, who was about 36 weeks pregnant at the time. 'Hi, Ben. We just wanted to know how Percy was?'

'She's dead, Katherine, she's dead.'

Silence.

Katherine called her husband – my younger brother, Robert – but he was in a lecture and his phone was in silent mode. She texted him. 'Call me.' Thinking of her pregnancy, he scrambled past everyone in the hall and went out to ring her back. 'Percy's dead,' Katherine told him and he immediately jumped in a cab and went home to her. An hour or so later he too rang Mum's mobile, not wanting to disturb me. Again, for some reason, I answered it.

Robert didn't expect to hear me and cried down the line, saying, 'I'm so sorry,' over and over.

'I can't believe she's dead,' I said to him again and again in response. I also said how sorry I was that I had told Katherine in the way that I had. I told him that having a baby wasn't meant to be like that and that she would be all right. A shock like this was hardly what Katherine needed when pregnant herself.

A little while later Tim and Christine arrived from the hospital. Our house had become the natural focus, but no one really knew what to say once there. And I felt so isolated. Even with people around me. So numb and alone.

Harry. I had to tell him now, not later at bedtime when he was due to come back. Where do you start with telling a three-year-old child that he would never see his Mummy again? Why did I have to break his little heart as well?

Mum had rung Jess, our neighbour, at 8 a.m. and had delivered him to her by 8.30. They had played in the park, been to a pizza restaurant for lunch and had a wonderfully happy day.

I rang Jess and told her over the telephone: 'She didn't make it, Jess.' I asked if I could come round and speak to Harry.

When I arrived Jess let me in, then quietly took her daughter, Jemima, out into the garden, leaving me with Harry who was sitting on the sofa watching *Teletubbies* on CBeebies. He looked up at me and beamed. My heart broke again.

'Harry, you remember Mummy had a sore tummy and Daddy took her to hospital so the doctors could try and mend it? They tried really, really hard to make Mummy better, but she was very sick, and they couldn't make it better.' What was I saying? 'Mummy was too ill, Harry, and now she's in heaven with God and the angels, and her tummy doesn't hurt any more.' He didn't know whether to watch the television or look at me. He just went so quiet and we hugged and hugged. He never said a word. I explained that he could stay for tea and a bath at Jemima's house and that I would come and collect him when it was time for bed. He liked that idea, so I took pyjamas and toothbrush round a short time later.

I listened to the message that Sally had left on my mobile earlier when I hadn't been able to speak. Chris had heard from my aunt, who lives in the same mews as the Coys showrooms, that Jessica had been put on life support and dialysis during the night. Sally was horrified that it had come to that. She couldn't believe it and was ringing to find out what on earth was happening. I called her back at 3 p.m. when she was outside school, waiting to collect her daughter.

'How is she?' she asked.

'She didn't make it, Sally.'

'What do you mean?' She didn't register what I was saying.

'She didn't make it,' I repeated.

'Oh my God. What happened?'

I explained what had happened. And I didn't cry this time – I think it still hadn't properly sunk in. We were both totally disbelieving of what I was telling her.

Sally called Chris to tell him and then Fiona. From that point the shock wave started to spread and nobody bothered me with the triviality of work after that. The support, on the other hand, kicked in immediately. Sally called or texted me virtually every day from then on. Just to listen. To comfort and to reassure.

```
From: Edward Bridger-Stille
To: Ben Palmer
Date: 30 June 2004 15:32
Subject: <no subject>

Dear Ben,
I heard the news, I am so so sorry. Jessica
was lovely.
Words seem meaningless at this stage but
Antonia and I are thinking of you.
Edward
```

Papa reached the house at about four o'clock with a suitcase for Mum. It had been obvious that morning that Mum would need to stay for at least a day or two, but he had been unreachable since then. I answered the door.

'How's Jessica?' he immediately asked. Bang. Here we go again.

'Papa, she's dead.' He stood on the doorstep, his eyes filling. It was the first time in my life that I had seen my father cry.

At some point in the morning Mum had taken Emily to the doctors' surgery because she had been a little snuffly and, as is the case with many babies, a bit jaundiced – no more than might be considered usual but with everything that was going on Mum wasn't taking any chances. They initially saw the health visitor or midwife at the walk-in baby clinic, but were referred on to a doctor. Dr Williams saw them immediately and was horrified by what Mum told her. Although she was quite happy with Emily, she spoke to the paediatric registrar at Kingston in light of what had happened and they decided that, if I wanted, they would admit Emily and test her for what the hospital by now knew was Group A streptococcus – purely as a precaution.

So around mid-afternoon I rang the paediatrician myself and arranged to take Emily straight in. I would have to go back to A & E. Cold sweats from the memories alone. Knowing my wife was somewhere in that building. In the mortuary. Shiver. I had to concentrate and hold it together. Emily needs you, I told myself.

```
From: Fiona Goulden
To: Ben Palmer
Date: 30 June 2004 18:38
Subject: <no subject>

Dear Ben,
I can't even begin to imagine what you are
going through — you must be devastated. Max
and I just wanted to let you know that, al-
though it is probably the last thing on your
mind right now, when the time comes there is
absolutely no question that both Harry and
your daughter will be welcome at Hurlingham
on full Bursaries. We would feel extremely
privileged to have them at the school.
All our thoughts are with you.
Fi and Max
```

As we crossed the car park towards A & E, I was again carrying Emily in her car seat. The wind was blowing all around us and as it changed direction, I swung Emily around so that the back of her seat would act as a shield. Mum commented on this later, but I guess it was instinctive – I had to protect Emily against everything. I was all she had.

We waited while the receptionist bleeped through that we had arrived. I stood there sweating. I doubt it was particularly hot; I was just so frightened and anxious.

Then Mum, Emily and I were met by the paediatric registrar and taken through to the children's ward. Emily was subjected to a full battery of standard tests, including a lumbar puncture, and blood was taken for analysis. She was then started on precautionary antibiotics and we discussed food for her overnight stay. I hadn't brought enough, but one of the nurses kindly said she would walk down to the chemist and buy more of the same brand we'd been using. I asked whether I should stay the night with Emily or not. Once again I was torn, my loyalties now split, as a single parent and I had to decide which child needed me more. Obviously it was Harry with his confused, broken heart. Emily's needs were being totally looked after in hospital and, as they said, I could call them to check how she was at any time in the night.

I gave the nurse some money for the formula, then Mum and I kissed Emily goodnight. I couldn't stand that both my girls were in the hospital together, yet a million miles apart.

As soon as I got home I went to Jess' house to collect Harry. Mark was home by then. Jess had called him, and he had dropped everything and gone straight home. When Harry heard my voice he came running out to see me. The expression on his face is one I will never, ever forget. It seemed to say: 'You came back for me, Daddy. It's all right, Daddy, I'm here. We're going to be OK; we've got each other, Daddy. I love you, Daddy.' How could there be so much wisdom in the face of such a small, innocent and confused child?

Both Harry and Jemima were in their pyjamas, running around and laughing, albeit that Harry was slightly more subdued than normal. I wanted to take him straight home, but he insisted on staying for a story. Finally, I took Harry home to bed and Jess and Mark told me I could go back later for a drink if I wanted.

```
From: Ben Palmer
To: Edward Bridger-Stille
Date: 30 June 2004 20:06
Subject: <no subject>


Thank you so much. Everyone is being so kind.
It is just so hard to understand.
Ben


From: Ben Palmer
To: Fiona Goulden
Date: 30 June 2004 20:08
Subject: <no subject>


Fi
You are both just so kind. Your whole school
is lovely. I just wish Jessica had seen it -
I just hope that somehow she can.
Ben
```

That evening, Mum was busy in the kitchen preparing some supper for both of us. I was sitting at the table watching her when I suddenly thought, this is all wrong, and found myself directing a violent verbal assault at her. Of course, she had done nothing wrong and was quite taken aback. But I just couldn't handle it – it was the wrong woman in our kitchen. In Jessica's kitchen, where she had organised the shelves and cupboards, put her lavender on the rail and arranged the cutlery drawer so that if Harry reached in it would be a spoon he pulled out first, not a knife. Mum was doing things the wrong way. Not Jessica's way. It felt like a desecration to me. But I knew I would have to get used to it. And that was what was so painful. Things were never going to be the same again. I broke down in tears and apologised.

Just before ten o'clock I rang the ward, to check that Emily was all right, which, of course, she was. Then I went along to see Jess and Mark. I don't think they had meant for me to go round that late, but they were still up, feeding their baby daughter. We drank a bottle of wine and talked for hours. I ran over events again and again. They were so kind and supportive and so obviously totally shocked themselves.

I came home at around 1.30 a.m. and spoke to Mum.

'I can't believe the love,' I said to her. The love that people were showing.

Then I went to bed. So, so alone. Our loss was only just beginning to sink in. What had we lost? Harry and Emily had lost their mother at the tender young ages of three years old and six days old. I had lost my best friend. My confidante. My rock. My wife. My lover. My raison d'être. My world. We had all lost our security, our confidence, our past and our futures. The three of us remaining had each other, though. Jessica had lost her life.

Day 8: Thursday, 1 July

From: Ben Palmer
To: Fiona Goulden
Date: 01 July 2004 09:55
Subject: <no subject>

I'm so sorry; I never said thank you. THANK YOU from the bottom of my heart.
Ben

From: Ben Palmer
To: Vanessa Marcais
Date: 01 July 2004 10:02
Subject: Baby Girl!

Ness, I have some very sad news. Jessica became very ill on Tuesday morning, and after a

long night in Intensive Care, she died yes-
terday lunchtime.
I'm sorry to be so blunt - I'd love to talk
more in the coming days.
Love to you all,
Ben

I rang the hospital again first thing. Emily had had a good night and she could come home.

By now, Laura was also camping downstairs on the sitting-room floor and she went with me to collect Emily.

We met the nurses in the paediatric ward and were told that the blood test results would be known later and that the registrar would telephone with them. Then we were taken through to see Emily. She was still lying in her cot in the little side room. She had a line in her, still connected to an automatic syringe full of antibiotics. It was the same type that Jessica had had so many of only the day before. It sent a shiver through me even though I knew that Emily was well. She looked so helpless and now she had just me to care for her. I had only the slimmest of idea of where to start, but I knew she needed me and that I needed her.

We drove home with Emily but found that the parking space outside the house was a little bit too small for me to park the estate car easily. Seeing a much larger space further along the road, I headed for it, saying to Laura, 'Life's too short.' We looked at each other, then, realising what I had said, we cried. I've always said it, and I said it a lot in the early days after Jessica died, crying each time I did so. Now I say it because I know for a fact that it is true.

We later learned that although Emily's blood had tested clear, they did find Group A streptococcus in a culture grown from a swab of her umbilicus. Ordinarily this would be ignored – many of us do have it on our skin – but a five-day course of antibiotics was recommended to be on the safe side.

That day was also Harry's sports day. Jessica, always so organised, had flagged it in the diary and we had all been looking forward to it.

Emma, Harry's much-loved nursery teacher, called for him on her way to school. Then, a little while later, Mum, Laura, Christine, my brother Charlie and I walked to the park and met up with the assembled children and other parents. The teachers obviously all knew that Jessica had died the day before, and word had already reached a few of the mothers we knew. Still, we stood in a slightly isolated group and looked out for Harry. Sitting in line with the rest of his team, he looked slightly bemused, wearing a borrowed green T-shirt to match his team colours and his baseball cap the wrong way round. I waved to him and he looked reassured and relieved to see us there.

It took a while for proceedings to get under way and I noticed that Harry was fidgeting. I walked over and whispered in his ear. 'Harry, do you need to do a wee-wee?' He shook his head, clutching his trousers. 'I think you might do, Harry. Shall we go over there?'

'No, I don't want to.'

'It might be a good idea, Harry, before the running starts,' I urged.

Then Harry relented. 'Yes, I do,' he said and we ran over to a tree together. He was absolutely bursting. It struck me then that we were like two little lost boys looking for a way through. So dependent on each other; both so confused.

I took Harry back to the Green Team and left him with a hug and a smile.

The races started amid great excitement and much encouragement. Harry was in the middle of his line and soon it was his turn to run the obstacle course. He really didn't want to do it – there were so many people watching and he was overwhelmed and muddled – but with lots of support from the teachers he walked the course, clutching his most beloved and constant companion, Bear. When he finished there was a massive cheer. He deserved it – he was so brave.

I heard one mother remark, 'Look at that shy little boy, isn't he sweet?' He's not shy, I thought. He's only three years old and his mother has just died. She wasn't to know.

To wind up the proceedings each child was to be presented with a participation certificate. The children were sitting in a semi-circle around Mrs B, the head teacher, when it started to rain. One insurrectionist wanted to break ranks, but Mrs B stood firm. 'When you've got your certificates you can go back to your mummies,' she stated. Not my boy, I thought. He was desperate to, but knew that he couldn't.

We left the park and walked home to have some lunch. Christine was walking beside Harry, avoiding the lines (so that the bears didn't come!). 'James James Morrison Morrison, Weatherby George Dupree . . .' she began. Then she stopped. She choked, unable to continue. The next lines are: 'Took great care of his mother, Though he was only three.'

After lunch, Harry had his customary rest in our bed. He was, unusually, lying on Jessica's side of the bed and Charlie sat on the other side talking to him.

'If you like, you can stay here with me,' Harry invited.

'Thank you, Harry – I would like that.'

Suddenly the wind blew the half-drawn curtain into the room, making the rings quietly clink.

Harry looked round, then back to Charlie: 'What was that?'

'It's just the wind,' Charlie reassured him.

'I thought it was my mummy. Because I've looked all day for my mummy and I couldn't find her.'

'No, because do you remember where she is?'

'She's in heaven with God and the angels.'

Harry had been practising our address with Mum and Laura earlier in the day, on the way home from sports day, so his next question should not have come as a surprise: 'What number is God at?'

'God doesn't really have a number,' Charlie said. 'But if he did, he would probably be at Number One.'

From: Sophie Crosthwaite, Gregor Fiskens
To: Ben Palmer
Date: 01 July 2004 13:15
Subject: x o x

Dearest Ben,

I just want to get in touch and say a big hello
and to say how devastated I am to hear about
the sad news. It really has thrown us in the
office and although we really don't know what
to say we really just want you to know that we
are all here thinking of you loads and loads.
I really hope that you are getting through
these couple of days and although we can't
imagine what you are going through we are all
here for you.
If you need us we are just around the corner.
Lots and lots of love,
Soph, Will and Gregor
X x x x x xx x x xx x xx x

On Thursday afternoon, after they had finished with sports day and
the afternoon session for those children who stayed at nursery all
day, Mrs B and Emma – Harry's much-loved teacher – dropped by
at the house, with flowers, cards and presents for Harry and Emily.
They didn't want to linger, but with Mum's help I managed to press
them into staying for a cup of tea.

Jessica had asked Emma to come and look after Harry during the
summer holiday afternoons so that she would have time to concentrate on Emily and hopefully be able to rest a little too. Of course
I was now very grateful to Percy for this arrangement, although I
hadn't been privy to any of the details, so I took this opportunity to
confirm with Emma when she would start working, what plans she

and Jessica had made and how much she was to be paid. She was to prove invaluable that summer.

Mrs B and the other teachers at nursery were so kind and helpful, particularly in the early days (the last week of term), having him for extra sessions and lunch if needed. Some mornings Emma collected him on her way in to school and he even had breakfast there. Mrs B also gave me special dispensation to drop Harry off and pick him up either early or late so as to avoid standing in the queue on the stairs which made me feel claustrophobic and panicky.

```
From: Alistair Brown
To: Ben Palmer
Date: 01 July 2004 17:15
Subject: Ben


Hi Ben,
What can I say?
I cannot imagine what you and the kids are
going through at the moment, but if I can do
anything at all, now or in the future, please
just give me a call.
I just can't believe I am writing this to you
now. To say it is unfair just isn't enough.
All I can say is try to stay strong, and I'll
speak to you soon.
Al
```

At some point during on that Thursday the Coroner's Officer telephoned me. I had been told he would by the hospital, but it was still a surreal conversation. We could have been discussing car insurance. He took, or rather confirmed, some details and told me that a post-mortem had been scheduled for the following day. Based on the findings, he explained, the Coroner would decide whether or not to hold an Inquest.

God, an Inquest: how traumatic would that be? He said he would call me to let me know the outcome of the post-mortem and told me that the full report would be available after a couple of weeks, and that I was entitled to request a copy. He suggested I might want someone from the hospital to take me through it. But I didn't want to read it – why would I want to know what each of Jessica's organs weighed?

```
From: Harry Palmer
To: Multiple Addresses
Date: 01 July 2004 20:30
Subject: Ben and Jessica

Dear all,
I am afraid I have to pass on some tragic
news. On Tuesday Jessica was taken into hos-
pital with severe pains. Her blood pressure
collapsed and her kidneys started failing.
She had a massive infection which the doctors
tried desperately to counter-attack but she
sadly died on Wednesday afternoon.
Her baby daughter, Emily Kate, has just spent
24 hrs in hospital being thoroughly checked
out to ensure she hasn't the same infection
but she is fine. Minette is helping Ben look
after her.
I am sure all your thoughts and prayers will
be with Ben at this time.
Harry

From: Irena Brewis
To: Harry Palmer
Date: 01 July 2004 21:08
Subject: Jessica
```

Dearest Harry,
A simply awful thing to have happen to you
all, and terrible to have to tell us all.
Hearts and prayers totally with you, Minette
and Ben.
With fondest love,
Irena & Bobby

Once again, after supper I went to see Jess and Mark. We talked about
Harry's sports day and we talked about Jessica. I told them about
how we had first met, and I flippantly said at one point, 'I suppose
one day I'll marry again.' I think the extreme shock had made me
so numb that I had somehow briefly managed a level of acceptance
that would take me a very long time to regain. It felt really good to
remember the happy times.

Jess kindly offered to tell our neighbours what had happened for
me. I was so relieved; I really didn't want to have to do it myself. I felt
such a failure; I had lost my wife – how careless was that?

From: William Brewis
To: Harry Palmer
Date: 01 July 2004 22:21
Subject: Ben and Jessica

Dear Harry,
We are both so shocked and upset for all of
you. Jessica was so vivacious, lively and
joyful, we can't really believe that she has
gone. There is nothing we can say of course
to make things less unbearable, but none the
less we should very much like to write to
Ben and express our sympathy and sorrow. We
have his email address but in the circum-

stances that seems unsuitable. Would you be good enough to let us have his postal address please?

We are thinking of you and praying for you all and send you our love.

William and Kalantha

That night Harry woke up and led me a merry dance, running between our bedrooms over and over again. I tried everything but he would not settle back down. It went on and on, my patience wearing thinner and thinner.

'Please, Harry, please get back into bed,' I begged him. 'Harry, I'm so tired. Please will you go to sleep?'

But nothing I said or did worked; we just wound each other up more and more.

Finally, I snapped. I crumpled on the floor beside his bed, sobbing, pleading with him to give me a break. I couldn't cope with any more. I was absolutely broken, physically and mentally exhausted and my nerves were now being shredded to pieces by a small boy who felt pretty much the same. Harry was stunned. Up to this point I had bravely worn a poker face and he must have thought that he was alone in missing Mummy.

This wasn't, by any stretch of the imagination, the last time that Harry was difficult or played up, but I think we reached an understanding that night: we were both aching and angry. It marked the beginning of a new bond that continues to grow more powerful every day. A bond of strength and loyalty between us – and Emily as well – that holds our lives together. Nobody should ever have to suffer like this, but we would do it together as a team, as a tight unit.

We were going to survive, whatever it took.

Day 9: Friday, 2 July

From: Ben Palmer
To: Alastair Brown
Date: 02 July 2004 00:16
Subject: Ben

Thanks Al.
The support I am receiving is phenomenal. It makes a massive difference at an extremely hard time.
I cannot begin to understand this, any more than Harry & Emily will, but while I have lost my wife & best friend, they have lost their mother at 3 years old and 5 days old respectively. I cannot imagine what effect that will have on them. Life can be a bitch - enjoy it while it isn't.
Ben

From: Ben Palmer
To: Sophie Crosthwaite
Date: 02 July 2004 00:23
Subject: x o x

Thank you so much; there is no way of understanding something like this and little that
can be said. It is so valuable, though, to
know how many people care. If Jessica could
see the number of messages in my inbox she
would be stunned. I am & always will be extremely proud of her: she has given me two
beautiful children. It just breaks my heart
that she is no longer here for them.
Ben

More and more, if Harry awoke in the night, or early in the morning, he would climb into bed beside me with his cold feet. Before long he would only go to sleep at night if he was in my bed. Jessica's bed. Our bed. I was setting a precedent that I would never previously have sanctioned, but it gave Harry comfort and security. And it meant I had my family around me. Emily in her cot, to my right and Harry, beside me, on my left. Both close enough to touch if it was me that woke up in the night. For comfort and reassurance.

I found that I couldn't bear for either Harry or Emily to be out of my sight, out of my reach. The impact of this feeling of need and insecurity was wide ranging. I didn't like anyone taking either of them away from me – grannies included. When one of the mums from Harry's nursery called by one morning and offered to take Emily out in her pram, I was horrified by the thought of it. There was no way I could let her go. It wasn't that I didn't trust her, although afterwards I realised that was probably how it came across.

It was hard to explain, but Harry, Emily and I were all that was left. We had to stick together and forge a new, tighter and stronger bond. This was always going to happen naturally, but I felt an overwhelming urge to force it. More for myself than for them, I think.

It is remarkable how easily children adapt to the worst of situations. I think it took Harry about a week to get back on track with his routine. As parents, we may feel devastated that we are not missed for longer, but we wouldn't want them to go through months of pain, anguish and heartache in the way that we do. And it wasn't as if Harry stopped missing Jessica altogether. Months on he would still say, 'I miss my mummy.' He still misses her every day, but his acceptance of his loss comes so much easier than mine, and he knows he is so, so loved. In a way I am envious, but I know that he will ask many questions later on in life, when he is ready. It may be that Harry's grief is a time bomb, ticking away quietly until some trigger in his life – exams, a new school or some other upheaval – detonates it. In the meantime, all I can do is love, support and nurture him and help his confidence to grow.

During these first days, a recurring thought was: How am I going to find a new wife? Who would want me? Everyone half nice must surely be married already. Will I have to wait for people to get divorced? This thought would very quickly be followed by immense feelings of guilt. I remember sitting in a traffic jam and bursting into tears. 'I'm sorry, Perc, I'm sorry. I love you. Forgive me,' I cried. I could not believe that she had been dead for only 48 hours or so and that I was already mentally trying to replace her. Of course I wasn't, though. I think it probably stemmed from a very normal fear of the unknown, of being alone.

So many of my early thoughts were confusing and some very upsetting. It was a violent roller coaster of emotions. Shock. Anxiety. Fear. Anger. Disbelief. Isolation. Panic. I found that I was also completely unable to make a decision about anything. I really didn't have a clue.

I developed a habit of sighing deeply and regularly, as if I was trying to shift a stone from my chest that was causing me physical pain.

'Don't do that,' Mum would say. 'You'll hyperventilate.'

'It helps,' was always my reply.

One day around this time, I went to the supermarket – just to get out. But halfway round I felt a choking panic sensation. I was sweating as I queued to pay and left but, in my hurry to escape, I had forgotten to pay for the car park and when I got to the bottom of the exit ramp found my way was barred. I became so uncharacteristically flustered I hardly knew myself. I tried to reverse up the winding ramp and met a car coming down. I was stuck. I had no idea what to do. I drove back down again and found then that the kiosk was manned. Bemused, the attendant took my £1.20 and I left, cursing both my stupidity and my reaction to it. I had a great deal to learn, I realised, about myself and about the state I was in.

On another occasion, walking along the pavement in Putney, I kept noticing people who bore a passing resemblance to Percy; whether it was the length, colour or style of hair, a similar jacket or blouse, the slightest thing, it seemed, would make my heart race as I looked then looked again. I began trying to find Jessica among the crowd. I simply could not believe what I knew to be true. There had to have been a mistake.

I don't think I ever 'searched' for Percy like that again, but for months afterwards I would see something about someone and think it was her. It was going to be so, so hard to escape the pain.

Walking home from the corner shop one morning I saw Richard, one of our neighbours, ahead of me. I slowed down – I didn't really want to bump into him. Relations between us and Richard and his wife, Mary, had not been great ever since we'd had a few arguments a year or so earlier about builders and their kitchen extension. I wanted to avoid him but he had clearly seen me.

'I'm so sorry, mate,' he said, as he got closer. 'Jess and Mark told us about Jessica.' Then Mary came out and hugged me.

'Look, mate,' Richard continued, 'I know things haven't been too easy between us, but if there's anything we can do for you . . .'

I knew he meant it and said to him, 'Richard, what's in the past doesn't matter any more. It's all insignificant now.'

Misunderstandings and disagreements like these just became so unimportant and trivial; both Richard and Mary have been very good friends and neighbours ever since, and I am grateful.

```
From: Ben Palmer
To: Annabel Nash
Date: 02 July 2004 10:30
Subject: Jessica


Annabel
You probably haven't heard, but Jessica lost
a fight against septicaemia on Wednesday. She
died a little before noon, after a brave fight
in intensive care. She had an infection nobody
knew about. Emily was born on the Thursday
before, and Jessica fed her & loved her for
4 days before going back into hospital.
I think she had lost touch with most of her
school friends, but she always meant to look
everyone up again one day. I'd be very grate-
ful if you could tell anyone you are in touch
with.
I'm sorry to break bad news like this.
Ben
```

On Friday morning the Coroner's Officer rang me back and I steeled myself for what he had to say. He explained that the findings of the post-mortem, which would be recorded on the death certificate, were that Jessica's death was caused by:

    (a) multi-organ failure (caused by)

    (b) septicaemia (caused by)

(c) post-partum Group A streptococcal infection.

I was told that I would be able to register Jessica's death at any time, as the death certificate from the Coroner would be with the registrar imminently. Also, that the Coroner had decided that there was no reason to hold an Inquest.

So there it was. I was so relieved. The thought of an Inquest was too much to bear – the possibility that something might have gone wrong. I just wanted closure, somehow.

Also that morning, and several times a week for the next three and a half weeks, the community midwife called by to see Emily, obviously having heard what had happened, and we talked quite a bit about the events of the previous few days.

I recall vividly her saying at one point, 'My profession must learn from this,' which seemed to echo something I'd already been giving a lot of thought to – that there must be some action I could take, in Jessica's name, to prevent the same thing that had happened to her from happening to someone else, to some other family. I had no idea what, but I knew it had to involve education, education, education. We talked about the idea and she agreed with a lot of what I was saying.

```
From: Annabel Nash
To: Ben Palmer
Date: 02 July 2004 11:58
Subject: Jessica


Oh my God, Ben
I can't believe it's true.
I know how Jessica felt about losing touch
with old friends. It is too easily done. But
the happy memories we all shared are worth
holding onto and remembering with joy.
I have great memories of our friendship. I
don't know if she told you that we had a joint
```

party together at her parents' house (before they split up). It was a fantastic party and I've still got a copy of the invitation! We must have been 16 and 17.

We had a great time in those days as she lived near me in Buckinghamshire and we were in the same house at Wycombe Abbey. My first and only round of golf was with Jessica at Denham Golf Club; I seem to remember some great parties at the clubhouse as well.

Jessica was always fun to be with, always laughing and smiling though we shared some of the same teenage torpor over parents divorcing and remarrying, etc. etc.

I'm sorry I didn't speak to Jessica again and she certainly won't be forgotten. I will of course let people know.

I'm so sorry for your loss Ben and please keep in touch, if you ever need to speak about her with someone, because I know from losing my mother that sometimes it's just good to talk about them with someone who's been through a similar experience.

My thoughts are with you and your beautiful daughter Emily and all the family.

With all mine and Tim's warmest thoughts at this painful time.

Keep in touch.

Annabel

After lunch, while Harry was having a nap, I decided to go and register both birth and death. I felt I just had to do it, despite Mum's concerns about my going alone. As I drove to Kingston and passed

Robin Hood roundabout, along that same route I'd taken to and from the hospital, I talked to Jessica.

'Please, Percy, come with me. I need you to be there with me, so I don't have to do this alone.' And, however strange it may sound, I really didn't feel alone; I felt totally capable of registering Emily's birth and then Jessica's death.

While I was waiting my turn I saw a list on the noticeboard in front of me of the most popular girls' names in the area for the last quarter. Top of the list was Emily; next was Jessica. How strange was that?

The Registrar was extremely sensitive; it turned out that for years she had lived in our street, at the end of the block. The poor woman had never done a double registration like ours before and had to ring someone to ask how to complete Emily's birth certificate as Jessica was dead. Thankfully, the answer was that because Jessica was alive at the time of birth and after it should be a totally normal registration. This did cause, however, a very tense few minutes. Finally, with the paperwork completed, I left, with a heavy heart.

I now had the documents to prove it.

The registration had taken longer than I'd expected and when I got home Harry was awake and anxious. He didn't know where I was and was fearful. Hardly surprising – Mummy was gone and now Daddy wasn't there either. Even though his gran was there to reassure him, he was very frightened. Ever since then I have gone to great lengths to explain to him where I am going, why I have to go and when I would hope to be back. It helps to assuage his concerns and the welcome I always get on my return is heart-warming, to say the least.

From: Henrietta Palmer
To: Harry Palmer
Date: 02 July 2004 14:21
Subject: Jessica

Harry,

That is such awful news. I am so sorry, you must all be absolutely devastated. I didn't know Jessica well, just saw her at her and Ben's wedding and family gatherings, but she and Ben were so happy together and that was really lovely to see. My heart goes out to all of you, to Ben especially, and to her family. Please would you let me have Ben's address so I can send him a card?

Love,

Henrietta

That evening, Christine came to the house. She came over quite a lot in the first few days. I think, understandably, it helped her to feel close to Jessica and her memories. But on this particular occasion Christine started a conversation that surprised me.

'Where will you move to?' she asked. 'Don't take the children too far away; they're all I've got left.'

Why on earth did she think I was going to move? Why would I want to? She was frightened and hurting, but didn't realise that our life was here. The most traumatic thing for a child following the loss of a parent is change. A move of house and/or school could actually be more devastating than the bereavement to someone of Harry's age. We were incredibly lucky in that we would not be forced to sell the house – the mortgage carried life insurance, payable in full on first death – and that we would not have to be uprooted.

The conversation then changed course. It was far too soon for either of us to react rationally, but Christine asked me what I had in mind for Jessica's funeral and burial or cremation. Jessica and I had never really made firm plans, but when we had discussed our deaths it was always in the context of me dying first in old age. Jessica had joked that she would just become a difficult old Scottish woman, ruling with a rod of iron (I think she had her paternal grandmother in mind as a role model) and I had wanted, should it be possible, to be buried at St Matthew's, Blackmoor – an hour down the A3 from our house and where my family come from. My great-great-great-grandfather built the church, the village school and a house for his family there. Jessica had said she would, of course, want to be buried with me when she died, but now there was a complete role reversal. Still, I was sure that Jessica would want to stick, more or less, to this plan.

I had already established that a plot would be available (if this was what I decided on) in the family area of the graveyard. I didn't want to even consider cremation.

Christine was distraught. 'But it's so far away!' she cried.

Did she want me to bury her daughter in some London cemetery, surrounded by strangers? I wondered. Or scatter her ashes to the wind?

The talk did not progress well and soon became an argument, largely, I think, because of the lack of any suitable alternative. I was angry because, while I would never have wanted to do something that was truly hurtful, I was Jessica's next of kin and funeral arrangements were quite definitely my responsibility. Jessica was a Palmer, and she was proud to be one. I felt it only fitting that she was buried in a Palmer graveyard, among family, as we had discussed.

Christine left that evening under a black cloud.

Day 10: Saturday, 3 July

On Saturday, Philip – who was Harry's godfather and a friend of Jessica's since childhood – and his wife, Karen, came over. They had telephoned the night before, which was fortunate, as a note in our diary that said, 'Phil & Karen to collect tickets' in Jessica's hand, meant nothing to me. They explained that they'd arranged with Jessica to use some of our parking passes as they would be watching Wimbledon that day.

They came early and were marvellously kind to me, both of them hugging me so tightly. When Phil came in he was strong and composed, all six-foot-something of him. But when he saw Harry, standing at the foot of the stairs he dropped down to hug him and his face just crumpled.

We all sat together, drank tea and cried. None of us could believe that this was for real. Then, when I took Emily upstairs to change and feed her Laura and Karen came up with me and we started talking about nannies. I just didn't know what to do or where to start. I didn't want a nanny. Neither Jessica nor I had ever wanted one; we'd wanted to bring our children up ourselves. Karen was really helpful, suggesting I look for a short-, medium- and then long-term option, making it so much easier to think about.

Phil and Karen had brought several children's books for Harry about bereavement and I was very touched by this. I had barely thought about what would be going on in Harry's mind and certainly didn't know how to begin to address it. The books would hopefully help make this task easier.

That same day, Mark came in from next door with his daughter, Jemima, and was met by Mum (who had taken up residence) in her rubber gloves. It was all hands to the deck! Mark kindly offered to take Harry out to the park with them, but I declined his offer. Still the shut down going on in my head did not want to allow anybody out of the house or out of my reach.

Day 11: Sunday, 4 July

From: Harry Palmer
To: Susanna Lyell
Date: 04 July 2004 09:56
Subject: Ben and Jessica

Dearest Susanna,
Some terrible news I have to pass on to you.
A week ago Jessica had a bouncing daughter,
Emily Kate, 9lb 13oz.
On Tuesday Jessica was taken into hospital
with severe pains. She had a massive infec-
tion and, despite the doctors' best efforts,
she sadly died on Wednesday afternoon.
Emily spent 24 hours in hospital being thor-
oughly checked out as a precautionary measure.
She is now on antibiotics but is home and
totally fine.

Minette and Laura are at Ben's house helping
with both children and I am popping up and
down with supplies, etc.
I am sure your thoughts and prayers will be
with Ben at this time.
With love from,
Harry

From: Ben Palmer
To: Alex Wilbraham
Date: 04 July 2004 20:22
Subject: <no subject>

Dear Alex,
Tracked you down via your firm's website! I'm
writing because you very sweetly got in touch
last time I put an announcement in the paper.
I now find myself in the position of being
about to place two simultaneous announcements, and wanted to let you know.
On Thursday 24th, Percy gave birth to a
beautiful girl, Emily, and proudly brought
her home the following day. Last Tuesday
morning Jessica became very unwell, and was
taken back to hospital by ambulance. She
was transferred from A&E to Intensive Care,
where she fought bravely through the night.
She had a major infection which caused septicaemia which, in turn, caused multi-organ
failure, and Perc sadly died just before
noon on Wednesday.
We were both very aware that we had receded

into our own little world of nappies & childcare, and hadn't seen any of you for a long
time, but always intended to get in touch one
day. I'd be very grateful if you could let
Joss know, or let me have his email address.
I trust you are all well; the girls must be
quite grown up now!
Love to you all,
Ben

Day 12: Monday, 5 July

On Monday morning I had several visitors, but one in particular was of immense help. Father Derm is chaplain at Laura's old school and a family friend. Before we were married, Derm (or possibly it was Mum) thought that Jessica and I should have some pre-marriage advice or preparation.

I remember how we had sat down in the sunshine at my parents' house, eagerly waiting for Father Derm to impart his great wisdom.

'Well, you guys have been living together for long enough,' he began. 'There's probably not a lot I can tell you. Do you like rugby?'

Our conversation today, however, was very different. We talked a lot, particularly about the thoughts I'd been having about finding a wife. His view on it was, 'Well, it's natural. When people are bereaved they often have a lot of thoughts that most people don't admit to. There are subjects that for some are taboo.'

I was so relieved to realise that I was still normal.

I telephoned April Richards, the vicar at Blackmoor, who had been expecting my call, obviously. We didn't know her very well, although she had baptised Harry and we always spoke to her whenever we went to church while staying with my parents. Still, she was so kind. I agreed to visit her on Thursday to discuss arrangements and she gave me the name of a local funeral director, David Leggett, whom she knew and trusted and whom I called next. He too was very helpful and I made an appointment to see him on Thursday as well. I also faxed him the 'green slip', authority for him to collect Jessica's body from the mortuary.

The funeral was arranged for eleven o'clock on the following Monday, 12 July. Papa's birthday.

There was so much to do, I hardly had a moment alone or to think. Thank heavens.

```
From: Alex Wilbraham
To: Ben Palmer
Date: 05 July 2004 14:25
Subject: <no subject>
```

Dear Ben,
Oh God, no. Percy, dear bright, delightful Percy. No, no, no. There is no justice, none. Dear, dear Ben, I cannot bear the thought that you should suffer so and your children, your poor children . . . Why does this happen to good, kind people? Why? God alone knows, but I am certain only the good have spirit to endure what is dreadful and not be broken. And you are good, Ben; one of the few truly good people I know. You have the strength and courage to face the darkest days and come out still yourself and still the kind of

father that any child is lucky to have. Your heart must sink as, God, I know mine would, to think of bringing children up alone. But remember, you have more to give your children than fifty lesser men. That is why Percy chose you and she chose well. But the terrible pain and loneliness; to have your dear Percy taken away. How monstrously unfair, how can anyone deserve this, least of all you? It makes me want to ask God for my money back.

But we are here, Ben. You are right to say that nappies, children, etc. can bury us sometimes; subdued, unsociable, sink-into-the-woodwork people that we are, but we all crawl out at times like these. Please count on us. Whatever your friends can do, they will do. Ask and we will do whatever we can, for you, for the children, for Percy whom we knew and loved and will miss so much.

I have told Joss and will look out for the announcements in the paper re. the funeral, etc. All our contact details are below. Please let me have yours again. Please let us know what practically we can do to help; in the near future or the long term. I imagine that you may be awash with family, etc. in the first few weeks but, as the days go by, things will thin out. The only practical advice I can offer is - please pester us - all your friends. You will suffer an awful lot on your own as it is but do not try to do it all alone. I know a thousand of your friends could not replace one Percy but we can sometimes take some of

the strain and you will need some time for
yourself.
I know it is trite to say that we are thinking of you but it is true. We are thinking of
you, the children and poor, dear Percy and we
always will be; that also is true.
Both Fernanda, myself and the girls send all
our love and deepest, deepest sympathy.
Alex

Christine came to the house again on Monday afternoon. We went
upstairs to my study to have some quiet. I wanted to gently raise the
subject of Blackmoor again. I explained that there was no way on
earth I wanted to cause any upset, but that I really believed it was
the right thing, and what Jessica would have wanted.

Christine agreed with me. I was incredibly relieved; it made
everything so much easier. I told her that a plot had been marked
out, in the shade of an enormous lime tree. Christine and I both
thought it sounded perfect.

Over supper with Mum that evening I learned that Tim had
spoken to Papa at length over the weekend, concluding by asking
what the 'admin' arrangements' were. My interpretation of this was
that he was clearly asking what I was doing and why there were no
funeral arrangements yet? I was incensed. What was I supposed to
have done? Jessica had only been dead a few days and already the
politics were getting far too complicated and upsetting.

In retrospect, I think that Tim simply felt left out and helpless.
I should probably have called him to talk and to explain what was
happening. But for a very long time it was extremely hard for me to
remember that I was not alone in my grief. I felt alone and could not
think beyond the three of us; even that was asking the impossible
on some days. I just didn't have the emotional or physical capacity.
Why did no one see that?

There is no rehearsal for being widowed in this way. It is not about acting logically or considerately; it's about raw survival. It is an immense challenge and you don't necessarily always get it right.

Day 13: Tuesday, 6 July

From: Susanna Lyell
To: Harry Palmer
Date: 06 July, 2004 06:44
Subject: Ben and Jessica

Dearest Harry,
What an absolute tragedy. Nick and I are
thinking and praying for you all so much and
especially for Ben.
I can hardly bear to think what you are all
going through at the moment. But how wonderful that Minette and Laura are with Ben to
help him with little Harry and baby Emily,
with you in support too.
Last summer I had such a lovely time at your
lunch sitting next to Ben and meeting his
darling little Harry. It is too cruel that

Jessica has been taken away from him, and just when they must have been so happy with the arrival of their beautiful daughter.

Veronica and Oliver are thinking and praying for Ben too.

Thank you for letting us know. We will be thinking of you all and we send you our deepest sympathy and love at this sad, sad time.

Susanna

Day 14:
Wednesday, 7 July

Birth announcements, The Times, Wednesday, 7 July 2004:

PALMER – On June 24th to Jessica and Ben, a daughter, Emily Kate, a sister for Harry.

Death announcements, The Times, Wednesday, 7 July 2004:

PALMER – Jessica Kate aged 34, tragically on 30th June after a sudden illness. Adored wife of Ben, devoted mother of Harry aged 3 and Emily aged 6 days, beloved daughter of Tim Percival and Christine Percival and much-loved sister of Kit. Funeral service at St Matthew's Church, Blackmoor, Nr Liss, Hants on Monday 12th July at 11.00am. Enquiries to Thorne-Leggett on 01420 488896.

From: Joss Wilbraham
To: Ben Palmer
Date: 07 July 2004 08:44
Subject: <no subject>

Ben,
Please forgive the use of email at such a time.
Alex passed on the very, very sad news. Ben, I am so very sorry. I'm sitting here in front of my PC at work trying to comprehend what you must be going through and frankly, I don't think I can. To use the hackneyed expression, sometimes actions speak louder than words. Suffice to say that Monday is blocked out and I will definitely be coming.
I know that this is not the right time to be talking about me, but given how hopeless I've been at keeping in touch, I'd like you to know that I've moved into a wonderful cottage in Oxfordshire with my girlfriend Fi and her three-year-old girl, Indigo. When the dust & chaos settles I would love to pick up where we left off and get you all down to stay for a loooong weekend; believe it or not I'm becoming quite a dab hand with little nippers (just survived Indigo's third birthday yesterday!). Please treat this as an open offer, along with the many others that I'm sure you have received.
Masses of love,
Joss

By the way, if you need any labour on Monday,
I've taken the whole day off.

From: Ben Palmer
To: Joss Wilbraham
Date: 07 July 2004 09:47
Subject: <no subject>

Joss,
Thank you. Very much.
Perc will be laughing at the thought of you &
birthday parties - our 3rd was pandemonium!
I really really appreciate your coming, as
will she.
Love,
Ben

On Wednesday morning I went back with Emily to see Dr Williams. There was nothing wrong with either of us, but I think she just wanted to make sure we were all right. We discussed many things, including Harry, and she agreed to refer him to a paediatric psychologist, just for my reassurance. Over the next couple of weeks she rang me several times – sometimes daily – to check that we were still doing OK.

I was still feeding Emily through the night and she demanded maximum attention. Of course, I had Mum and Laura to help who were marvellous, and although I refused their offers initially, they did have Emily downstairs in the 'girls' dorm' with them for four nights, so that I could sleep through.

Dr Williams had offered to give me something to help me sleep if necessary but, to be honest, I was always so exhausted that sleep came relatively easily. She would also frequently say, 'And alcohol?' to which I would be tempted to reply, 'Yes please'! She was concerned that I might be drinking too much. I wasn't – not then. Mum and I would share a bottle of wine between us at supper and that was about it. Quite restrained, looking back.

From: Ben Palmer
To: Joss Wilbraham
Date: 07 July 2004 16:17
Subject: <no subject>

I was just rereading your email & saw the bit about labour and that got me thinking. While I can't immediately think of anything sufficiently strenuous, I wondered how you'd feel about a reading/short poem? Personally, you wouldn't get me up there, so would totally understand if you didn't fancy it, but it would be great as you did introduce us all those years ago!
Ben

Things were very busy around now. Harry had to be dropped off and collected each day, there was shopping to be done, Emily needed huge amounts of attention, letters and emails were literally flooding in and, on top of it all, I was trying to organise a funeral for the following Monday. Telling everyone when and where it was to be was a job in itself.

Word of Jessica's death had spread far and wide at a phenomenal rate. For some reason I was terrified that nobody would come to the funeral, although when I actually sat down and discussed it with Mum, we realised that we may have to cater for upwards of two hundred people.

I agonised over Harry. I felt he had every right to be at his mother's funeral, but given his confused state of mind, feared that he wouldn't understand, may be troubled by seeing 'grown-up'

125

grief and might well have nightmares about seeing a coffin buried. Should you take a three-year-old boy into the emotionally charged atmosphere of his mother's funeral? I just didn't know. I wasn't hiding the facts from him, but was trying to keep his life on as even a keel as possible. I hope he will agree with my decision when he is older.

In the end I arranged for his lovely Emma to come down with us for the day and look after him at Burhunt during the service and afterwards. I explained to Harry that all of Mummy's friends would be coming for a party to remember her, which he thought was a very exciting idea. 'Is Mummy coming?' he asked, his big eyes looking up at me. Oh God, I thought. Help me.

Day 15: Thursday, 8 July

In the morning, I drove down to Hampshire and met David Leggett. We discussed all aspects of the funeral's logistics: hearse, limousine, pall-bearers, flowers, the list was endless. Jessica had only ever said one thing about her funeral: she wanted her coffin to be drawn by four horses with magnificent black plumage – it was the Georgette Heyer romantic in her. But I had always told her that this was far too East End gangster for her and that if I was around to plan it she wouldn't have them. Sorry Percy, I thought, I'm going to stick to my word. And at least she would have known I would.

But I needed to choose a coffin. And it had to be the best. No question: solid oak and brass handles.

Mr Leggett asked me whether I would want to view Jessica's body again. The shock of this question shut me down momentarily, without my knowing quite why. But then I told him I wouldn't – I had seen her shortly after she died and felt I had said as many goodbyes to her as I could. I have tossed and turned many a night since then about whether a few more minutes with her body would have been helpful, but I think not. What has occurred to me is that, as I have often heard, she would no longer have looked like my Percy because of the undertakers' processes. At least when I did see her last she looked like the girl I loved. Just.

While I was with Mr Leggett, his office telephone rang twice, both times in response to the notice in the newspaper. They had already had a huge number of enquiries. The estimate of two hundred plus now wasn't as ridiculous as it had seemed. The church would be full.

I then went on to meet April at the vicarage. She was so kind, as she always is. We talked a lot and then addressed the issue of the service. I had chosen some hymns and had made a selection of poetry. April helped me along with a good steer and suggested a reading. We ran through the service and finalised details, then agreed that I would prepare an Order of Service and email the finished artwork to a local printer who would print it over the weekend and deliver it to the funeral directors first thing on Monday morning. No room for error.

I arranged readers and asked Phil to speak about Jessica. He was the obvious choice having pretty much grown up with Jessica as family friends, and being godfather to Harry too. He did caution, 'Are you sure? I may cry.' Perfect. Honest and true. We both knew it wouldn't be an easy thing for him to do, but I wanted him to know that it was OK and that he should just get through it any way he could.

I remembered to pick up my suit from the dry-cleaner. I bought new shoes, a white shirt, a black tie and got my hair cut. For you, Percy.

That evening I typed up the Order of Service and Laura and I edited and double-checked it all. Then I emailed the artwork over to the printers. Mum meanwhile had gone home earlier in the day once I got back from Hampshire, to get everything ready. In two telephone calls a day or two earlier she had organised a marquee for the garden – the forecast was for rain, booked the caterer, chosen food and arranged for a florist to provide flowers. She was marvellous.

I'd noticed in our diary – a *Dodo-Pad* in which each day is divided into five columns (one each for me, Jessica and Harry plus a spare and one for general events, birthdays, weekend-away plans) – an entry in Harry's column for that day. In Jessica's loud handwriting was written, 'Picnic 11 a.m.–1 p.m.' I never did find out where, or with whom. There were also entries like '3.00 swimming' on Thursdays that I just couldn't deal with – I knew they had just started going to a new place but I didn't know where or who to contact to cancel it. I just had to leave it. I figured that if something really mattered, someone would call.

In the garden of the house two along from ours there were two huge fir trees that were growing rapidly. The house had recently been sold and Jessica and I had desperately hoped that the new owners would cut the trees down as they took a large area of sun away from our garden for most of the year. I think it was around this time that the tree surgeons did indeed come to fell them and as the lower branches of the first fir were being cut, the wind caught just the very tops of the trees. I swear it was Jessica, dancing with glee.

Day 16: Friday, 9 July

My cousin, Matthew, came down from his house in north London to see me and in the evening the two of us went to the pub around the corner. It was still sunny and warm so we sat outside on the pavement, drinking our cold beers. We talked about what had happened, about Jessica in happier times. We got a couple more rounds in and talked more and more. As the sun went down and the evening drew in it got cold, so we moved inside. I went to the loo, and when I came back to the table, I found Matt crying. I was slightly taken aback, but he, along with everybody else, minded so very much.

Eventually, we staggered home. We had had a few too many beers, shed some tears and had some laughs. That was going to become something of a pattern.

Back at the house Marian gave us some supper – a chicken casserole she had brought up with her. (She had arrived in the morning to stay and help, taking over from Laura who followed Mum to Hampshire.) Then Matthew left and made his way up the road to Southfields tube station. He told me later that as he had rounded a corner, tears flowing, he'd passed a man and almost bumped into him. 'Don't worry, mate,' the man had said. 'There's plenty more fish in the sea!' I know that if anyone had said that to me I would have hit them although I suppose it was not an illogical assumption that Matt had been jilted.

Day 17: Saturday, 10 July

In the morning I drove Harry and Emily down to Hampshire with a heavy heart and a hangover.

The weekend was busy. Marquees went up, tables, chairs and ovens for the caterers were delivered, Papa and I mowed the lawns and the flower beds were tidied. Burhunt was full, busy and being made ready. For Jessica. She would have been so embarrassed that so much effort was being made for her. But you are family, I thought. Everybody loves you.

At some point in the day I went down to St Matthew's Church. I wanted to look at the plot before the funeral. As I walked around the corner of the church I saw a mini-digger and two men. Oh no. No, no, no. They were digging the grave right now, I realised. I retreated. Then, taking a deep breath, I walked around the corner of the church again and approached the grave. They stopped digging.

'Was she . . . Are you—?' began one of the men.

'Yes,' I said. 'She's my wife.'

He was so kind. He came over and told me he'd heard about what happened and asked was the 'babby' all right. Then he apologised for being 'not very good at sympathy and that'.

'That's all right,' I told him and smiled. 'Just so long as you can dig a good grave.' He put a hand on my shoulder. He was very good at sympathy – far better than he knew.

Day 18: Sunday, 11 July

There was to have been a huge family picnic in my aunt and uncle's house a mile along the road on Sunday. Jessica and I had been looking forward to it. She had said, even if she didn't feel up to going because of Emily, that Harry and I should definitely go. It was family. Family really mattered in Jessica's eyes. In the event, as soon as my uncle, John, realised that Jessica's funeral was likely to be the next day, he postponed the party. It didn't occur to me that he would, but I was really touched by this gesture. He is another person who showed me immense kindness and has given me terrific support.

After the bustle of preparation, Sunday was different. The house was full and Harry was busy, playing with toys, running around the garden and marvelling at the enormous tent. I was quiet, though.

The organisation had kept me focused over the past few days and provided a slight distraction, but the reality was still there. I was alone with two tiny children, desperately missing Jessica and still in shock from her death.

Looking Laura or Mum in the eye meant that one or both of us welled up, but we talked. About Jessica, her plans, her joy at having a daughter. And we reflected on the fun that she and Emily might have had. I found it an inescapable train of thought, but one that did little for my mood.

After supper I had a glass of whisky, then went up to bed. To the double spare room that Jessica and I had always used when at Burhunt, since just before we were married.

We had always been put in separate rooms until a week before our wedding. Jessica had gone to bed early, while I had stayed up talking to my parents about weddings and honeymoons. When we eventually retired, I headed for my normal bedroom but Mum stopped me at the top of the stairs. 'No,' she said, 'you're in that room.'

'But we're not married,' I replied, embarrassed, but teasing her slightly.

'As good as,' she said, smiling. 'Night night.'

I'd climbed into bed, in the dark, trying not to disturb Jessica, but she woke up. 'What the hell are you doing? Your mum'll kill us!'

'I don't know – she told me to use this room!'

Then we'd giggled, like a pair of naughty teenagers.

Lying in the same bed now, imagining Jessica's hair on the pillow beside me, I cried myself to sleep.

Day 19: Monday, 12 July

Monday morning came. I was so nervous. I had butterflies in my stomach. How on earth was I going to get through the day? Christine had suggested, more than once, that I should take something to calm me, but I felt outraged. I wasn't ill; didn't need medication. The day was obviously going to be hard, but I wanted to experience it with honest emotions, whatever they were to be.

The past week had been so busy with plans and preparations, I had been totally absorbed. It all had to be just right for Jessica. It was the least I could do for her. It was the last single thing I could do for her. After this, we were on our own.

Suit on, tie straight, stand tall.

People started to arrive. Then the limousine arrived. The driver gave me two envelopes from the funeral director.

The first read simply:

> *3 locks of hair of the late:*
> *Mrs. Jessica Palmer.*

I had asked for these for the children and me. The full impact was now starting to hit home.

The second was a letter from someone who had written to me care of Thorne & Leggett. I didn't know them and they didn't know me, but it was a truly beautiful letter. Several people – strangers – had written to me having read the announcements in the papers. So many people had been deeply affected.

We drove down the hill to Blackmoor in silence, and the car pulled up behind the hearse. The coffin looked splendid, adorned with the huge arrangement of flowers I had ordered. Splendid? What was I thinking? This was my wife in her coffin – how could that be splendid? What was this? What was going on? I was overwhelmed with emotion, confusion and grief. I bit my lip to try and recover myself before we entered the church.

Everybody got into position and the coffin was gently lifted out and up onto the shoulders of the six pall-bearers. I followed immediately behind, with Emily, barely three weeks old, in my arms. Dramatic? I hoped so. But mostly I was holding her because it would, I hoped, force me to retain a modicum of composure, knowing that I couldn't drop her. I realised now that despite wanting to feel the raw emotion, I was terrified of going to pieces and missing the service.

We slowly crunched up the gravel path and wound round into the church. I couldn't take my eyes off either Emily or the back of Jessica's coffin. Eyes straight. But then I was hit by the swell of a wall of people on each side, as they turned to Jessica's coffin. There was the rustle of people crossing themselves as we processed slowly up the aisle. The church was absolutely packed. Standing room only. They're all here for you, darling, I thought.

Jessica's coffin was lowered onto two trestles (borrowed from the funeral directors apparently as the church's own had wood-worm and hadn't yet been replaced. The coffin could not have been heavy – she was so small – but the thought of it crashing to the floor in a cloud of woodworm dust was not a good one.

On the inside cover of the Order of Service I had printed:

Friday's child is loving and giving

Jessica was, without a doubt, all three. I followed this with some ABBA lyrics. Jessica loved ABBA, and although I'm not sure if she knew these particular words they seemed so appropriate:

> *Dance while the music still goes on*
> *This is no time for crying*
> *Dance, don't you hear them play our song*
> *God knows that we've been trying*
> *Dance while the music still goes on*
> *Just like the night I met you*
> *Dance and believe me, when you're gone*
> *You know I won't forget you*
> 'Dance (While the Music Still Goes On), ABBA, 1974

Then the organ struck up and we stood.

> GUIDE me, O thou great Redeemer,
> Pilgrim through this barren land;
> I am weak, but thou art mighty,
> Hold me with thy powerful hand:
> Bread of heaven,
> Feed me till I want no more.
>
> Open now the crystal fountain
> Whence the healing stream doth flow;
> Let the fire and cloudy pillar
> Lead me all my journey through:
> Strong deliverer,
> Be thou still my strength and shield.

> When I tread the verge of Jordan,
> Bid my anxious fears subside;
> Death of death, and hell's Destruction
> Land me safe on Canaan's side:
> Songs of praises
> I will ever give to thee.

The church fell silent after we'd sat down, and Jessica's aunt, Joanna, walked up to the lectern and read:

> Then I saw a new heaven and a new earth; for the first heaven
> and the first earth had passed away, and the sea was no more.
> And I saw the holy city, the new Jerusalem, coming down out of
> heaven from God, prepared as a bride adorned for her husband.
> And I heard a loud voice from the throne saying,
> 'See, the home of God is among mortals.
> He will dwell with them;
> They will be his peoples,
> And God himself will be with them;
> He will wipe every tear from their eyes.
> Death will be no more;
> Mourning and crying and pain will be no more,
> For the first things have passed away.'
> And the one who was seated on the throne said, 'See, I am making
> all things new.' Also he said, 'Write this, for these words
> are trustworthy and true.' Then he said to me, 'It is done! I am
> the Alpha and the Omega, the beginning and the end. To the
> thirsty I will give water as a gift from the spring of the water of
> life. Those who conquer will inherit these things, and I will be
> their God and they will be my children.'
>
> Revelation, chapter 21, verses 1–7

Joss, who had been there when Jessica and I had met, then took Joanna's place. In a faltering voice, he read the poem that I had emailed to him.

Life Goes On

If I should go before the rest of you
Break not a flower
Nor inscribe a stone
Nor when I am gone
Speak in a Sunday voice
But be the usual selves
That I have known

Weep if you must
Parting is hell
But life goes on
So ... sing as well

Joyce Grenfell, 1910–1979

The words echoed around my head, and I blinked away a tear as Phil stepped up. He had worked hard on his eulogy, calling me to confirm details, as well as spending an evening with Tim to fine tune his words. I hoped that there would be some happy memories and that the lighter side of Jessica would come through.

Jessica

Jessica, Jess or Percy, as she was known to her many friends, meant a lot of things to a lot of people. To quote but a few she was: loyal; a wonderful listener; selfless; loving; utterly foolish; caring; strong.

To me, Jessica – and I apologise to those of you who knew her as Jess or Percy; in the same way that only my parents and Jessica ever called me Philip, I have to call her Jessica.

To me, Jessica was great fun, a little bossy, a good laugh with that shocking laugh, irrepressible.

My first memories of Jessica go back to when we were young children – running riot at Mayfield; walking in the woods at Burnham Beeches; swimming in the river Chess; the Christmas party at the golf club; golf lessons en masse with John Sheridan.

Jessica was born on 22 May 1970 and began her schooling several years later at Maltman's Green. As you'd expect she excelled, making friends at every turn. Her achievements, other than getting into Wycombe Abbey – which more than surprised a few – included her swimming and her acting, having once played the lead fairy in the school play.

In 1982 she moved on to Airlie House at Wycombe Abbey. It was at about this time that Jessica and I began to write to one another – Jessica and her endless supply of friends proving something of an attraction to me. I'm particularly sad to say that I haven't found any of the letters. I'd love to have seen the look on her face if I had.

Jessica's achievements at Wycombe included – joint house games captain, a key member of the house lacrosse team and house monitor. One I still find hard to believe – the school 2nd bridge team – notching up a memorable victory over Eton.

Although never officially rusticated, Chris [Christine] was called in by the headmistress, on more than one occasion, to discuss Jessica's conduct and her fluent story telling.

As one of her friends beautifully put it – 'Her main achievements were of the kind her friends would value but her house mistress wouldn't!'

Even so, Jessica left Wycombe with A levels in maths, history and economics and went on to read Earth Sciences and Geography at Royal Holloway College. Whilst the course may not have seemed a natural fit for Jessica, the frequent field trips to Spain and Scotland certainly were.

As always she made many friends and was a dream housemate. Not only keeping the house spotlessly clean but also insisting that her fellow housemates eat an orange a day – to keep them regular. She played lacrosse for the university and even found time to graduate with a 2:2.

Jessica best summed up her time at school and university saying to Chris – 'Just think what I could have done if I'd worked!'

Jessica's career, like her life, was colourful. Fittingly, it all started out with an ad' in the *Evening Standard*, that simply read: 'Are you young, enthusiastic & up for a challenge?'

She was. And the next thing she knew she was at Coys, auctioning classic cars.

She retained this upmarket feel, moving on to work at Sotheby's, Louis Vuitton and latterly with Chris, for Peter Lilley. To quote her boss from Coys, Jessica was 'irrepressibly cheerful and a rock in a time of crisis'.

It was while she worked at Coys that she and a colleague decided to take one of the cars for a spin down the Cromwell Road. It was typical of Jessica that the car in question was the original Batmobile – rocket and all. When the police eventually caught up with them, it was only down to Jessica's charm that they weren't arrested!

But none of these events changed her life. It was Ben who did that. They met for the first time on 12 February 1993 in, where else, but a pub in Fulham. It was six years later, almost to the day, that Ben popped the question and, just for once, Jessica was speechless.

They married on a gloriously sunny day in July 1999.

Harry was born two years later. All of Jessica's previous achievements were at once overshadowed by her brilliance at being a mummy.

She was patient and calm; she never complained; nothing was ever too much trouble. She and Harry knew how to have fun – she was a truly fantastic and loving mum.

I was lucky enough to see Jessica twice in the month before Emily was born. For a tiny person, she really was enormous.

She was convinced that she was going to have another boy but so desperately wanted a little girl. At almost 10lb she got far more than she could ever have wished for. All her dreams had come true – a perfect family.

One thing Ben told me that personifies Jessica more than any other, was when she was taken into hospital shortly before she died.

Despite being critically ill, her only concern was not for herself, but for Harry and Emily. She insisted that Ben be at home when they woke up in the morning.

We have all lost a great friend, but Tim and Chris have lost their only daughter. Kit has lost not only his sister but his best friend.

Harry and Emily have lost their mummy and Ben has lost the girl that he loves.

I am heartbroken but I know that if it had been different, Jessica would be standing here – strong – looking for a way forward. I'd like to end with a short quote from Alexander Solzhenitsyn:

Some people are bound to die young.
By dying young, a person stays young forever in our memories.
If they burn brightly before they die, their light shines on for all time.

Jessica, we will never forget you.

Philip Irons

Tears rolled down Phil's cheeks as he spoke. It was from the heart. Then, with great dignity, Jessica's cousin, Gavin, reminded us of why we were here, and how we should try to keep up our humour.

She Is Gone

You can shed tears that she is gone
or you can smile because she has lived.

You can close your eyes and pray that she'll come back
or you can open your eyes and see all she's left.
Your heart can be empty because you can't see her
or you can be full of the love you shared.
You can turn your back on tomorrow and live yesterday
or you can be happy tomorrow because of yesterday.
You can remember her and only that she's gone
or you can cherish her memory and let it live on.
You can cry and close your mind,
be empty and turn your back
or you can do what she'd want:
smile, open your eyes, love and go on.

Anon.

We stood again, and the organ struck up its powerful notes. I cried
as we sang:

O Lord my God!

O Lord my God! When I, in awesome wonder,
Consider all the works Thy hand has made,
I see the stars, I hear the rolling thunder,
Thy Power throughout the universe displayed.

Then sings my soul, my Saviour God, to Thee,
How great Thou art! How great Thou art!
Then sings my soul, my Saviour God, to Thee,
How great Thou art! How great Thou art!

When through the woods and forest glades I wander,
And hear the birds sing sweetly in the trees;
When I look down from lofty mountain grandeur,
And hear the brook, and feel the gentle breeze.

And when I think that God, His Son not sparing,
Sent Him to die, I scarce can take it in
That on the cross, my burden gladly bearing,
He bled and died to take away my sin.

When Christ shall come with shout of acclamation,
And take me home, what joy shall fill my heart!
Then shall I bow in humble adoration,
And there proclaim; my God, how great Thou art!

We remained standing as we prayed with April and listened to the Commendation. Then she read a Traditional Gaelic Blessing that Tim had asked for:

May the road rise up to meet you:
May the sun shine always on your face:
May the wind be always at your back:
May the rains fall gently on your fields and gardens:
And until we meet again, may God keep you
In the hollow of His hand.

Anon.

We stood for the final hymn. As we began to sing, I picked up Emily and held her tight.

ALL things bright and beautiful,
All creatures great and small,
All things wise and wonderful,
The Lord God made them all.

Each little flower that opens,
Each little bird that sings,

He made their glowing colours,
He made their tiny wings.

The purple-headed mountain,
The river running by,
The sunset and the morning,
That brightens up the sky;

The cold wind in the winter,
The pleasant summer sun,
The ripe fruits in the garden, —
He made them every one;

He gave us eyes to see them,
And lips that we might tell
How great is God Almighty,
Who has made all things well.

It was a beautiful service, not that I noticed all of it. There I was, sitting in the left-hand front-aisle seat, looking at Jessica's coffin covered in flowers. This was all so wrong. I just hoped that the service was all right.

During the last hymn, 'All Things Bright and Beautiful', we moved out to the graveside. It took an age for everyone to get out and assemble around the grave. Several times April encouraged people to move round and come closer, making space for others. There were people everywhere, in every available space between graves. I stood at the front, alone with Emily; everybody else hung back from us.

With the flowers removed to the graveside, I could now see a brass plaque on top of the coffin:

JESSICA KATE PALMER.
AGED 34 YEARS.

Too much reality. Too enormous for me to understand even now, I thought, twelve days after Jessica has died. But twelve days are nothing; it takes months and months. Maybe years.

'We therefore commit her body to the ground; earth to earth, ashes to ashes, dust to dust; in the sure and certain hope of the Resurrection to eternal life,' April read. Then David Leggett picked up a handful of the dark, sandy earth that gives Blackmoor its name and I heard it fall, crashing onto Percy's coffin. The sunlight filtered through the overhead leaves of the lime tree, and everything was quiet.

My chest shook and tears flowed. I could see and hear tears all around me. I whispered to the coffin again and again, 'I love you. I love you, Percy.' Part of me wanted to jump onto her coffin and tell her that she should come back. Part of me wanted the ground to swallow me up. I wanted to swap places with Jessica. If I could have died in her place I would have done. She shouldn't be dead. The children needed her so much; they needed their mother. I needed her so badly.

When she had finished the committal, April came over to me and I thanked her.

'Stay as long as you like,' she said. I stood for a bit, but we were finished here for now. I could also feel over four hundred eyes burning into me. I felt choked and panic-stricken. I turned around with Emily, but my way was blocked.

'I have to get out,' I whispered to someone – I think it was one of Jessica's aunts – and the assembled body of people parted like the Red Sea. I went back round to the front of the church, tears streaming. I passed the other flowers, laid along the path as I walked, and the wreath I had ordered on Harry and Emily's behalf jumped out at me. Even though I had written the card myself, it still felt like a knife in my heart. I had written only one word: 'Mummy'. Harry had scribbled his mark on it.

We drove back in the limousine, I think probably in one long convoy of cars. Anybody trying to pass through the narrow, sunken lanes in the opposite direction must have been horribly frustrated.

Once back at Burhunt, Laura gave Emily her bottle and we put her down for her sleep. Then we headed for a glass of rosé. Jessica always enjoyed rosé, particularly in the summer, as I'd said the week before when Mum and I were making plans with the caterer. Yet again, Laura and Mum were fantastic and looked after Emily for the rest of the day. Harry held court in the sand pit, with Emma and Mrs B in attendance along with countless others. Wonderful Mrs B had driven Emma down and stayed to help all day.

People were milling around on the lawns. It was like a marvellous summer party. Except that it wasn't. But it was a time for happy memories not tears. Laura had had a beautiful photograph of Jessica blown up to poster size, and it stood proudly on an easel, watching over us. Papa had taken it in Cornwall years ago at a house overlooking Polzeath beach. She was reading and hadn't been aware of the camera. It was Jessica looking thoughtful, serene, beautiful. She wasn't always serene – more usually she was bubbling with ideas and plans and never stopped talking. In this photograph, though, she looked truly serene with the evening sun shining through her long hair. I have a copy of the same picture above my desk, beside a photograph of Harry aged about eighteen months and an antenatal scan of Emily sucking her thumb. Such a Jessica thing to do – she never gave up thumb sucking.

I spoke to so many people, I lost track and lost count. There were people from every walk of Jessica's life, her family, my family, family friends, childhood friends, school friends, university friends, an ex-boyfriend, friends from nearly every company she had ever worked for, our neighbours, NCT friends and mums from Harry's nursery. So many people liked her, loved her and would sorely miss her. I don't think she realised how many. She'd have been so embarrassed.

We all saw a lot of people cry for the first time that day. I laughed and I cried. I was totally swept up in it. 'Thank you for coming,' I said, again and again. But I meant it. It meant so much. It was a great tribute to a great person.

The rain that had been forecast never came and the marquee was barely used, except for later, by Harry and a remote-controlled racing car.

Afterwards, when everyone had left and all was quiet, I stood in the garden with Laura, my hands gripping the back of a chair. Laura felt she had lost an older sister. Both of us were in floods of tears. Both struggling to understand what had happened and why. It was silent in the garden, such an anticlimax. I ached for Jessica and needed to be near her.

I ran upstairs to put on a pair of jeans, then drove back to Blackmoor. The grave had been filled, the mound of earth covered with all of the many flowers and wreaths. It was beautiful.

I cried for Jessica. I cried for Harry, for Emily and for myself. Tears were streaming down my face as I bent down and gathered up all the cards from the flowers; there were dozens and dozens and I kept dropping them, there were so many. Among them I found an invitation from Jessica's sixteenth birthday party attached to a posy from Annabel – it was the one she had mentioned in her email to me. Sixteen. So young and so much to look forward to. Her whole life ahead of her.

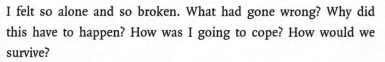

I felt so alone and so broken. What had gone wrong? Why did this have to happen? How was I going to cope? How would we survive?

I was very much in shock – I had been white as a sheet for most of the day – but it began to dawn on me now that, as little as I wanted it to be, this was the start of a new life. The old one was behind us.

A part of me had died with Jessica.

As I was told later, a friend of Jessica's had said after the funeral, 'For all of us this is closure. For Ben, this is where it starts.' This was so true. So painfully true and so frightening. As C. S. Lewis wrote about the death of his own wife, 'No one ever told me that grief felt so like fear.'

Many years ago, just after I left school, I had my palm read. I don't recall most of what was said, but I do remember being told that although I would live to old age, a break in my life line showed a major, life-changing event. I had always thought that maybe I would fall critically ill, but make a full recovery. I could never have imagined an event as shattering as the one I was now going through.

```
From: Simon Kidston
To: Ben Palmer
Date: 12 July 2004 17:13
Subject: <no subject>


Dear Ben,
It's hard to know what to say at times like
this so I'll just say what comes to mind. Like
you, I can't believe that Jessica is gone. As
a father I can't begin to express in words my
sympathies for your son. Life sometimes seems
so unjust when the most bubbly people with so
much to live for are those who are taken from
us early.
Jessica was great fun and I'll always remem-
ber her tone of voice, her laugh, our so-
cialising outside the Queens Arms all those
years ago (where have they all gone?) and
her reminding me of once throwing a diction-
```

ary at her for taking down wrong dictation!
We had fun, and knowing her will always be a
privilege and bring back memories of happy,
carefree times.

No doubt you will forge a new life for yourself and find happiness again, and I'm sure
your children will grow up to be people of
whom Jessica would have been proud. One of my
oldest friends lost her mother in childbirth
- she has turned into a beautiful woman with
everything to live for. I hope you can rebuild
your life and be strong, as your children will
need you, and even in this darkest hour you
must remember that you have a long life full
of opportunity and happiness ahead of you. I
wish you well.

Yours,

Simon Kidston

Day 20: Tuesday, 13 July

From: Phil Irons
To: Ben Palmer
Date: 13 July 2004 08:59
Subject: <no subject>

Ben
Jessica's address attached. I loved doing it,
it was just a pity there were so many stories
I had to leave out!
If there is anything you need us to do, please
do not hesitate to call any time and I mean
any time.
We'd also love it if you could all come for a
trip with us on the river. How are you fixed
for either Saturday 14th or 21st or Sunday
22nd August? Let us know.
Thinking of you,
Phil

It was around this time that I discovered the WAY Foundation – Widowed And Young – for which the only membership criterion is that you are widowed under the age of 50. I got in touch with the foundation soon after I read about it; it was – and still is – an enormous help to know that I am not alone, that there are people in a similar situation, and that they understand. Nobody else really does; it has to have happened to you for you to truly understand the depth of pain and anguish caused. Nothing else compares.

```
From: Alex Wilbraham
To: Ben Palmer
Date: 13 July 2004 15:31
Subject: Hi


Dear Ben,
I can hardly express my admiration for the
way you coped with yesterday. Extraordinary.
You had obviously put a great deal of thought
into how things were done and it was very
touching. Percy would have been proud.
On a practical note, as you may have forgot-
ten in the hubbub of yesterday, I am more
than usually available over the next month.
What I thought I would do is tell you when I
am around and then, if you want help/company/
errands running or whatever, you can just ring
me or send an email. I am baby/toddler trained
(double diploma), can cook, wash, etc. and
make a reasonable stand-in au pair (although
my t*ts aren't great). Please ring. I will
quite understand if you don't. You may have
a great deal of domestic help - mothers-in-
law, etc. - to look after Emily and Harry, but
```

I could also take you out for a beer if you like.

I am available this weekend, Friday evening, Saturday, Sunday. Evenings all of the week after (19-23 July). Saturday 24 and Sunday 25 (except Saturday evening when I have a birthday party in south London). There is a chance that I will be away on business between July 27 and 31. The evenings of August 2-5 are currently empty. My dad is coming to stay with me on the weekend of 6-9 August. The evenings of the week after are empty. In fact, as I write this I am beginning to see myself as a bit of a billy no-mates.

In the second half of August, when Fernanda is back, I am planning to take a week off. We may go down to the mothers in Beaulieu or just stay at home. Either way, it would be good to see you and the children then.

Just ring if you feel like it. Don't worry if you don't.

Love,

Al

After 'Where It Starts'

I stayed at Burhunt for a couple of days, then we returned home to London in time for a meeting with Max and Fiona at their office to discuss their IT requirements for the new school building that was now well under way.

Fi had called me to confirm the meeting and also to suggest that I may like to meet their nanny, Ali. Fiona explained how the day after Jessica died, she and Sally had sat together crying in Sally's car outside her son's nursery school. Both of them had two children (a boy and a girl each) so they could fully appreciate the enormity of the task that lay ahead of me and desperately wanted to find a way to help. Then Fiona had hit on an idea: 'Ben needs an Ali,' she said. Ali (Alison) had lived with Fiona and Max for the past five years, looking after their children and becoming a fifth member of the family in the process.

Fi thought that while they were away on holiday, Ali could look after Harry and Emily. Very quickly, though, she changed her plan and told me that if I got on with Ali, she would find someone else, totally freeing Ali up for us. So the planned meeting was moved to their house in Putney so that Ali and I could meet.

When I arrived Fiona hugged me. The look in her eyes said more than a thousand words ever could. She moved their second car so that I could park outside and had even bought a parking ticket for me. She doesn't stop at anything, and thinks of everything. Fiona is a truly amazing person.

The three of us discussed networks, servers, software and schedules and agreed an outline plan for the extensive new computer system I would install. Then they left me to meet Ali and talk.

I had never interviewed anyone in my life and with Fiona's recommendations I didn't really feel there was any need to. The question really was whether we would be able to work together. Bearing in mind my outburst at Mum in the kitchen, I was concerned about how I would react to someone taking over Jessica's maternal role. We had never wanted a nanny, never needed one, and it was an alien concept. However, I could see there was no choice. I was barely fit to look after myself properly, let alone a three-year-old boy and a newborn girl.

Ali and I talked for about an hour, during which time it transpired that her sister had been stabbed to death at home, by her husband, in front of their two children. I thought I had a tragic story to tell. How horrific was this? Fiona had told me that Ali's sister had died and that this might make her particularly suitable as she would understand some of my pain and why I might be moody, monosyllabic or just difficult.

We discussed arrangements, hours and how the house needed to run. She would work from 8 a.m. until the children were in bed at 6.30 or so. I hated bedtime. It always came at the end of the day, just when I was most tired, least able to cope and probably at the end of my tether. Also, as every parent knows, it is usually the time that a small child decides to get totally overexcited and throw a tantrum. Because our house wasn't big enough for a live-in nanny,

Fiona had said that Ali could continue to live with them, which seemed to suit everyone.

Ali was clearly totally competent, efficient, and unflappable. Flexible and relaxed as well. There was no question: she would start as soon as she could. I came away extremely relieved.

When I rang Fiona to thank her she said she would make a call that evening to see if she could arrange a nanny for her children, and then let me know. True to her word, she rang me that same night and said, 'Ali can start on Monday.'

Thank you. Thank you.

```
From: Ben Palmer
To: Alex Wilbraham
Date: 15 July 2004 23:09
Subject: Hi


Al
Thank you. I will ring (if I don't please
hassle!) and I'd love to take you up on kind
offers. Have just landed myself a Mary Pop-
pins, so future suddenly seems much more
bearable, and would love to go for a beer,
or get you here for supper.
Will try to call tomorrow or early next week
(back to parents for Saturday pm/Sunday).
Big thank you again.
Ben
```

Around this time, we were visited at home by the paediatric psychologist from St George's, who came to assess Harry, highlight any concerns and give advice. She wasn't sure what to expect when she arrived, but having taken one look at the terraced house and the domestic organisation she decided that Harry was happy and stable.

She talked to me for a long time though, focusing on whether or not I was coping.

When she left she said, 'You know where I am now, so if ever you're concerned about Harry you can get in touch.'

It was reassuring in itself to know that Harry was holding up as well as any boy might. I worried about being up to the job of providing the support he needed, but have always felt that we should approach our pain and grief as a family, and that unless I was getting something very wrong, we should be allowed to get on with it. The psychologist's assurances gave me the confidence to continue.

On Friday, two NCT mums, Nicky and Fiona, visited, bringing food, hand-me-down clothes for Emily and welcome hugs. I have always been a fan of hugs, but now, more than ever, they were taking on a new meaning. There is so much comfort in a big bear hug, and it was something from Jessica that I was sorely missing.

The following morning I took Harry and Emily to Chris and Sally's house. They had seen that there was to be a Peter Pan day in Kensington Gardens, and had bought us tickets, saying, 'You can come if you feel like it, or not. We'd like you to.' Initially I had resisted. I just didn't know how I'd cope. I didn't want to go, just wanted to stay in our cocoon, but I slowly came round. We'd be safe with them beside us.

We had some lunch and discussed plans for getting there. Someone suggested getting the bus. There was no way I was getting on the bus though with Harry, a pram and Emily. Even with help. The thought terrified me. So we drove in convoy and found parking spaces on Queen's Gate.

The place was heaving. I was sweating and extremely anxious. My head hurt and I felt like I was drowning. I nearly backed out of the whole thing, but Chris and Sally kept me going.

The park was full of fun fairs, side shows and people. So many people. I was on the verge of panic when we got into the throng. I was pushing Emily in her car seat on a pram chassis and was terrified of letting Harry out of my comfort zone – about a metre. Chris and Sally's children, Beth and Henry, were wonderful about taking him under their wings. We walked the course a bit, looking at the various Peter Pan areas, the fairy's garden, the pirate ship, and the Lost Boys' camp. Poor little lost Harry, I thought.

I couldn't look at anyone. I felt as though I wore my grief like a scar across my face. Gradually though, I settled, but my panic and anxiety was always just around the next corner.

When we all felt hot and tired and had had enough, we walked out of the park and drove around the corner to have a drink in the sunshine outside the pub opposite Chris' business.

Later that evening I drove down to Burhunt for the weekend. On Monday the next phase in our survival plan would begin.

```
From: Fiona Goulden
To: Ben Palmer
Date: 18 July 2004 19:42
Subject: General


Hi Ben!
I understand from Sal you had a nice time at
Peter Pan park yesterday.
Hope all goes well with Ali tomorrow. I am
sure it will. If you have any queries about
how to handle anything (although you proba-
bly won't) just phone or email me. We are all
delighted that you are in such good hands.
Take care
LOL,
Fi
```

From: Ben Palmer
To: Fiona Goulden
Date: 19 July 2004 20:30
Subject: General

Ali is fantastic. I really can't thank you all enough.
It all feels a bit strange, but a tonne weight has been lifted off!
Love,
Ben

From: Fiona Goulden
To: Ben Palmer
Date: 19 July 2004 20:58
Subject: General

I am delighted to hear it went well - it is always a little awkward at first, even under normal circumstances. Just go with the flow - she really is very competent and will only want what is best for Emily and Harry - sometimes you have to be a little cruel to be kind but trust me she will do it in the nicest possible way and your children will respond positively - it is usually easier when you are a little at arm's length; Hugo & Georgia were often a lot more receptive to her than to us! What you need from her is not only for her to give them love and affection but also a sense of order and structure which I would imagine will be a little difficult for you at the moment.
By the way - slightly awkward - I haven't

planted a spy in the house but understand Ali was legitimately looking through diary today and apparently it's Ben's birthday tomorrow - would that be Ben Palmer?
Fi x

From: Ben Palmer
To: Fiona Goulden
Date: 19 July 2004 21:43
Subject: General

I couldn't have put it better myself. Ali is fantastic; I just hope we're not too shambolic for her!
Jessica was efficient to the last - yes it is my birthday, BUT I would really rather it wasn't ;)

From: Fiona Goulden
To: Ben Palmer
Date: 19 July 2004 22:21
Subject: General

She is used to shambolic!
HAPPY BIRTHDAY!
Love from us all,
Fi x

From: Fiona Goulden
To: Ben Palmer
Date: 20 July 2004 07:54
Subject: HAPPY BIRTHDAY!

Good Morning.
HAPPY BIRTHDAY AGAIN!!!
The Gouldens

From: Alex Wilbraham
To: Ben Palmer
Date: 20 July 2004 09:43
Subject: Hi

Dear Ben,
I know that you probably do not feel like celebrating anything. In fact, this birthday has probably entered the top ten list of the world's worst birthdays, right up there with the Berlin Bunker Birthday of April 30th 1945. But, what the hell, more than ever you need a pat on the back for everything you are doing. So, Happy Birthday, all your friends are thinking of you. I am looking forward to seeing you on Thursday.
Love,
Al

From: Ben Palmer
To: Alex Wilbraham
Date: 20 July 2004 09:51
Subject: Hi

Yes, not my best one! Really rather it wasn't. Thank you, though. How on earth did you know?
Ben

From: Alex Wilbraham
To: Ben Palmer
Date: 20 July 2004 10:03
Subject: Hi

Someone I met at the funeral mentioned it. In fact, come to think of it, July 20th was also the day they tried to blow up Hitler and land on the moon - though not at the same time.

My birthday was truly awful. I wished everyone would just forget. What on earth did I want to celebrate for? Jessica had marked it in the diary, which was a painful reminder of her absence. I know, though, that I would have been just as upset, maybe more, if no one had mentioned it. I was full of contradictions, but ultimately needed to know that people were thinking about me, and about us. That whole week was so muddled and so painful, but I was being kept busy, and that helped.

Sometimes I would stand in Harry's bedroom looking out of the window at the garden. Jessica's garden. Although I helped with digging and planting and offered my ideas, she was the driving force, the planner. The houses in the next street back onto our garden, and you can see people getting on with their lives through the windows:

children in their bedrooms; people doing chores; mothers cradling their babies. It was so unfair. What right did they have to be alive and so happy, when our life was in pieces? I couldn't bear the injustice. Strangely, I have only ever really felt this strongly about people I didn't know.

Mummy and Papa and then Christine all visited in the afternoon and Robert, my brother, came in the evening. He and I talked a lot and about the events of Jessica's death. Up until now I had totally excluded thoughts of any mistakes having been made. I was totally focused on the fact that both the A & E and ICU had done everything possible to save Jessica. They had. I just hadn't thought back, before that point. I hadn't thought that her illness should have been noticed sooner. Robert, a barrister, had. Actually, a lot of people had. Some had mentioned it but I had just refused to listen; others had been too wary of causing distress.

The fact that so many had been talking so much behind my back about what I could/should do made me angry. This was our life, our misery, and I was going to go at my pace. However, if someone thought it wasn't the right pace, I wish they would have talked to me direct. But that evening, Robert did broach the subject and, to some extent, I again switched off. Certainly, my memory of our conversation is very faint, but, truthfully, that was probably the wine. He said he would do some research and come back to me.

From: Minette Palmer
To: Ben Palmer
Date: 20 July 2004 22:40
Subject: Nothing in particular

Darling - just to say you are the best dad in all the world. And we couldn't wish for a better son in all the world.
We send you all the love in the world. We think

of you constantly and will do anything in the world for you. Just click your fingers.

We'd love to babysit for you - on a regular basis. It's so easy to get to you. We can bring our supper and watch the telly (with or without company!), and you can have evenings out with your mates/neighbours.

We loved meeting Ali; she seems so very nice.

Hugs and kisses,

xx Mummy & Papa

From: Ben Palmer
To: Minette Palmer
Date: 21 July 2004 00:12
Subject: Nothing in particular

Thank you, & thank you for coming up. I think Ali will prove to be good news. After 2 days she has lifted a tonne weight from my shoulders & I have every confidence that that will continue.

xxx Ben

As well as my birthday, Jessica had also written in the end column of the *Dodo-Pad* for Saturday, 24 July: 'ANNIV'. We would have been married for five years that day. In the evening we would have eaten home made burgers and chips and drunk champagne and white wine. It was a tradition. On our wedding night we had stayed in the Waldorf in the Aldwych and eaten burgers and chips with champagne on room service. On the last night of our honeymoon, after two wonderful weeks in the Loire valley, we did exactly the same in The Lanesborough. They were the most expensive burgers we'd ever eaten.

Investigation – Part One

A couple of days after the conversation with Robert, I went for a pub supper at my local with Alex. As we left the house, with Ali babysitting, I saw one of my neighbours, Adrian, walking up the road towards us on his way home.

'Hi, Ben, how's the baby? We hear crying every now and then.'

Shit. Hell and damnation. It was three weeks since Jessica had died and no one had told him or his wife. I looked down at the ground, willing it to swallow me up, before saying, 'Adrian, I'm sorry nobody's told you, but Jessica died a few weeks ago, just after Emily was born.'

Adrian's face fell immediately, his embarrassment matching my own. I hated telling people like this. It always made them feel uncomfortable and all I could do was apologise. I felt as though my grief was tattooed across my forehead, yet somehow nobody else could see it. Why were we in this situation now? Please, somebody, couldn't we turn the clocks back, just once?

When we got to the pub we sat in the small garden at the front with pints and a menu. It felt good to get out of the house again, still within the safety zone of Southfields and with a good friend. We talked about how day-to-day life was, and about the still very raw shock of Jessica's death.

Then, very tentatively, Al raised the subject of negligence. He is a solicitor and had an extremely good grasp of the situation, but nevertheless my hackles rose. He explained that he had been approached by a family member at Jessica's funeral and had agreed to do some groundwork and then speak to me. Once again, I was annoyed by the knowledge that people had been discussing me behind my back. I told Al that I couldn't cope with suing anybody; that it would be too traumatic and confrontational and that I just didn't have the energy for it. Still, he persisted and asked me to let him outline the position as he saw it.

Al described how slow the law is and how much time there would be. In any event, he said, a solicitor would have to investigate the case first to ascertain whether or not there was a case to answer. But, as he put it to me, at least by investigating I would know the full story and the whole truth of what had happened to cause Jessica's death, and when the children were older they could ask any question they liked, and I would hopefully have an answer for them. If I didn't, they would – rightly – be very angry with me for not having uncovered the reason why they had no mother.

Having convinced me, Alex told me that in his view, as deaths like Jessica's were once so commonplace, but are now so rare due to advances in medicine, it was very likely that negligence could have played a part.

I was intrigued by Al's reference to negligence – I had been puzzling over the officially recorded cause of Jessica's death and, having done some research on Group A streptococcus infection and maternal death, I'd been appalled at what I'd learnt. Jessica died of what is now called puerperal fever, but used to be called childbed fever. It was an eighteenth-century disease. Why was a modern-day mother dying from something for which the cause had been discovered in the nineteenth century and the cure – pencillin – in the twentieth? I needed answers and Al's suggested course of action might well provide them.

He had already been in touch with a barrister friend, who often defends cases of negligence, and had asked him which solicitor he would least like to be up against. Without hesitation his friend answered, 'Claire Fazan.' Al had looked her up and confirmed to me that she was 'Mercedes' class. With my permission, he said, he would be pleased to contact her on my behalf.

'If you're a solicitor, and you're going to help me, shouldn't I pay you a retainer?' I asked him, tongue slightly in cheek.

'Absolutely,' Al went along with it, 'about a pound should cover it.' I handed over my pound and we set about ordering a pint of prawns and some lamb.

```
From: Alex Wilbraham
To: Ben Palmer
Date: 23 July 2004 10:47
Subject: <no subject>


Ben,
It was good to see you last night. I have
left a message with Claire Fazan to ring me
and will let you know when I have heard from
her. I hope Harry got off to his party OK.
See you later.
Al

From: Ben Palmer
To: Alex Wilbraham
Date: 23 July 2004 11:10
Subject: <no subject>
```

Yes, a good evening - although head a bit woolly this a.m.! Thank you so much for all your help & advice.

Definitely think the investigation is a must. Have talked it through with Mum this a.m. as well. She says she has spoken to 2 doctors (one is family, one a retired friend) who both think there HAS to have been negligence. I sort of don't want it to be the case, but we must know, and if there was they must be made accountable. If only to draw attention & maybe save one other mother.

See you later.

Ben

From: Alex Wilbraham
To: Ben Palmer
Date: 23 July 2004 11:36
Subject: <no subject>

I think you are right, Ben. The truth may be painful but, in the end, you (and later the children) will probably get more 'closure' out of knowing than by speculating for the rest of your lives. Looking for the truth is the right way to start. Money is a secondary concern and in moral/emotional terms it is a very inadequate remedy but it can, at least, bring security, stability and independence; all of which could help you do your job better.

In the newspaper today I read an article about a man (not Peter Touche) who has just

received £1 million from (the insurers of)
Basildon Hospital because his wife was not
properly monitored after giving birth to
twins and died. One should avoid thinking two steps ahead, we don't yet know the
truth but the size of these damages does
show how seriously the courts view these
things.
I'll speak to you later when I have spoken
with Claire Fazan.
Al

From: Ben Palmer
To: Alex Wilbraham
Date: 23 July 2004 11:48
Subject: <no subject>

I can think of better ways to get your name in
the paper. Hadn't thought about that aspect.
As you say one step at a time.
Shower rail fixed (at last).
Ben

Out of the blue, or so I thought, having largely forgotten our conversation, I had a long email from Robert. He had done a huge amount
of research and had sent me his findings, reinforcing the case for a
solicitor and an investigation. I had totally forgotten our conversation
of just a few days earlier and was embarrassed to admit it. I really
had put away a large volume of wine that evening. It was reassuring
to know, though, that the greatest legal minds of my friends and
family were singing from the same sheet, and I felt encouraged to
press on.

Al spoke to Claire Fazan and, having double-checked our diaries

– well, mine wasn't exactly full – we arranged for Claire to come to my house for a meeting on her way to the office a few mornings later.

```
From: Alex Wilbraham
To: Ben Palmer
Date: 23 July 2004 12:44
Subject: <no subject>

Ben,
All sorted for Wednesday 28 July at 9 a.m.
I will be there as well. One thing which
would be helpful for me to do tonight is to
check your household insurance policy. This
may cover legal expenses and, if it does,
it would be another funding option in addi-
tion to legal aid. Could you remind me if I
forget?
See you later.
Al
```

The following Tuesday, Al arrived at my place with two large carrier bags from the supermarket and cooked us a fantastic dinner. We talked through how the following day might go, and what I should expect, and after a couple of bottles of wine between us, I made up the camp bed in the sitting room for him and we turned in.

In the morning, when Claire Fazan arrived, I made tea and coffee, feeling rather awkward about having a Mercedes sitting at my kitchen table and thinking how embarrassing it would be if I was wasting her time. But she was kind and friendly, almost in an aunt-like way, and not at all what I had been expecting. She explained who she was, what she did and asked me to tell her, at my own pace, what had happened.

As I recounted the events from Emily's birth, through illness and death, she wrote notes steadily, only interrupting me once or twice to clarify a point. When I got as far as standing beside Jessica's grave, she stopped me. 'I'm sorry, Ben,' she said. 'This is painful for you. I don't need you to tell me about this part.'

I felt awful. I had been fighting tears and had just relived Jessica's death in a more detailed and complete way than I had – other than in my head – since it happened. I felt shattered. Little did I know how many more times I would have to do it, again and again.

Claire told me how she would, if I instructed her (and I wasn't to do so until after she had gone and I had thought about it), proceed, firstly, by establishing why there had been no Inquest when there were strong grounds to have held one. She explained how the investigation would be run and how it could be financed – partly through legal aid for the children and, hopefully (having looked at my household insurance policy), partly through my family legal protection cover. She also warned me to expect long periods of silence, but equally times when we would be in constant contact for days at a time.

When Claire left, over three hours later, I was exhausted. How little idea I'd had.

The first thing I said to Al was, 'Thank you so much – she is fantastic. How soon can I instruct her?' Together we drafted an email which I sent a very short while later.

From: Ben Palmer
To: Claire Fazan
Date: 28 July 2004 15:39
Subject: Jessica Palmer

Dear Claire,
Thank you very much for your time this morning, and for outlining the options available and the possible outcomes.
I would like to instruct you as we discussed,

and am forwarding copies of the documents you
requested by post. When you have had a chance
to read these, I would be very grateful if you
would contact Direct Line and the Coroner on
my behalf. Please also proceed with requesting
Jessica's records from the hospital, the GP
and any other necessary sources.
I look forward to hearing from you.
Kind regards,
Ben Palmer

From: Claire Fazan
To: Ben Palmer
Date: 28 July 2004 16:28
Subject: Jessica Palmer

Dear Ben,
Thank you very much for confirming your in-
structions so promptly.
As soon as the documents arrive I will press on
with contacting Direct Line and the Coroner. I
will send you a form to sign authorising re-
lease of Jessica's medical records to me.
Kind regards.
Yours sincerely,
Claire Fazan

In early August I received a draft copy of the statement that I had
made to Claire. It was accurate and in my words, but laid out in a
formal and emotionless way. I read it through, as though I was
hearing it for the first time, in tears. I was also sent legal-aid applica-
tions for Harry and Emily, which I signed as their 'litigation friend',
and a release form for all of Jessica's medical records, from birth to

death. That really made it feel final, even if I did continue to look up at the sitting-room window every time someone walked past, or a car pulled up.

Claire confirmed, first verbally and then in writing, that my insurance company would cover my third of the costs of the investigation. They kindly waived their normal requirement for me to complete a claim form, accepting instead just a certificate of death. She also wrote to the Coroner for South West London, requesting confirmation and an explanation of the decision not to hold an Inquest. Claire's letter – formal and business-like in tone – prompted the Coroner to telephone to find out why Claire thought there should have been one. Apparently, the Coroner had not been made aware of any concerns about Jessica's health before she had been discharged. There was an awful lot she didn't know, it emerged, so Claire put the record straight and, with my permission, she forwarded a copy of my draft statement. The Coroner promised to request copies of Jessica's notes and post-mortem report and to review her decision. As copies of these would also be going to Claire, she said that she would forward them on to me as well, although she assumed I wouldn't want to receive a copy of the post-mortem report. I agreed that she was right, shuddering at the thought.

I had resisted all thoughts of Inquest and legal action in the beginning because I was convinced that everything humanly possible had been done for Jessica after her re-admission to hospital. I still felt that. But I was coming out of shock now and could see that people were taking what had happened very seriously from the point of whether it should ever have got that far. A determination to know the truth and make sense of this catastrophic loss of life was growing within me. It also gave me another purpose to keep fighting on through day after day. If, as we suspected, negligence had played a part in the death of a wife and mother, then somebody was going to be held accountable. How dare they let her die?

I owed to it Jessica and to our children to find out.

Friends and Weekends Away

From: Ben Palmer
To: Guy Walters
Date: 02 August 2004 14:40
Subject: Hello

Guy,
I was thinking about Russell the other day
- mainly because I saw a fantastic lookalike
- and tried to call him, but am getting number
unobtainable. Is he still at 189 or has he
moved? Could you let me have a phone or email
for him?
Must catch up one day!
All the best,
Ben

From: Guy Walters
To: Ben Palmer
Date: 02 August 2004 21:09
Subject: Hello

Ben

How nice to hear from you! Attached are Russell's contact details.

He's working at *Arena*, the men's magazine . . .

How are you? Where are you? How many of you are there? We are three, and living in Wiltshire . . . any good for you?

G x

From: Ben Palmer
To: Guy Walters
Date: 03 August 2004 10:14
Subject: Hello

Guy

These are strange days: we still live in SW18 & have a boy, Harry, who was 3 in early June. Percy gave birth to a (very large) girl on 24th June - Emily. Our dreams had come true: more of the 2 than the 0.4 luckily, but the perfect unit: total bliss. We were on cloud 9. Until Perc became unwell with a variety of seemingly unconnected symptoms. On Emily's 5th day Perc was taken back into hospital where she continued to become extremely ill. She died the next day of multi-organ failure caused by a group A strep infection & septicaemia. There's no easy way to tell the story, but equally I can't pretend it isn't there. Sorry to send such news.

Love to you all,

Ben

From: Guy Walters
To: Ben Palmer
Date: 03 August 2004 10:40
Subject: Hello

Ben,

I'm so very sorry. I was talking to Annabel about you and Perc last night, prompted by your email. I was saying that you and she were a great couple, and how I regretted not being in contact with you, and hadn't seen you both for yonks. Perc was such a great girl, and you must miss her dreadfully. Anything I write will sound crass I suppose, but it's hard not to resort to cliché when one hears such shocking and tragic news.

I can't imagine how you are managing, but I expect the Palmer resourcefulness is having to kick in in a way that one could never have expected. I trust that the grandparents have waded in and I expect you are staying with one of them at the moment? I do hope Harry is coping too - it must be unbearably tough consoling him when you have so much of your own grief to deal with.

How are you filling your days at the moment? I expect you are trying to keep as busy as possible. If that is so, then please feel free to drive the 1hr 40mins down here to Wiltshire, where a vast amount of lamb and wine will await you. It seems silly to be attempting to renew contact at such a time, but, well, it's a sincere offer, and it would be lovely to meet Harry and Emily if you wanted to bring them.

Much love, and deepest sympathies,

Guy x

From: Ben Palmer
To: Guy Walters
Date: 03 August 2004 10:56
Subject: Hello

Guy

Thank you very much. I would really love to take you up. We're at home, going through the motions of 'normal' life. I have a super nanny who looks after the children, and makes sure I eat and sleep! Grandparents were brilliant, but it was quite nice to extricate myself from them all.

I have the fullest diary I have ever had - somebody for supper every night, and visitors (usually mums & toddlers/babies) during the day, which helps prevent the quiet and empty times, but it only ever runs to 4 or 5 days ahead. Large quantities of lamb & wine sound too good to be true; what would suit you best?

It is a funny time to renew old acquaintances as you say, but when something like this

happens you realise that we don't have all
the time in the world, and that friends are
really important, as is maintaining contact.
Something that Perc & I were very aware that
we were crap at!
Love,
Ben

The emails between Guy and I passed backwards and forwards many
times over the next 24 hours, as Guy cajoled me out of my comfort
zone and persuaded me that it would be easy to get down to them,
that they had plenty of baby paraphernalia, lots to do, much food and
a well-stocked wine cellar. So we made arrangements for the three of
us to go and stay with them for a weekend, a week and a half later.

From: Tom Russell
To: Ben Palmer
Date: 05 August 2004 09:04
Subject: Hello Bezza,

Sorry not to reply sooner, I've been off
school.
Walt told me your terrible news. I was
thinking about Perc just the other day and
what fun she was. A girlfriend of mine who
met her didn't stop going on about her for
days afterwards. My first memory is of her
running barefoot through my flat in the summer
of '91 when Sue Hope was cooking her 21st
meal; she was so very spirited and fun; but
you know that. I can't believe it. So sorry
to hear it. Her legacy at least looks you
in the eye every day and the time will come

```
when you can enjoy memories without so many
tears; I hope that day is sooner than we
all realise.
I'm so sorry, once more, but life will never
be this bad again - it's played its highest
card.
Tom
x
```

On the morning of 14 August, friends of Christine came to collect our dog, Annie, to take on holiday with them for ten days. Then, with Emily fed, the three of us were just about ready to set off for Wiltshire.

Ali had packed clothes for the children the evening before, so I loaded suitcases, travel cot, pushchair, bottles, steriliser, changing mat, nappies and wipes and a thousand things I didn't really need into the car. It took me over an hour to get everything in, to check I hadn't left anything out, then check again.

Even getting the children into the car was an ordeal. I struggled to get them both out of the door – Emily in my arms and Harry holding my hand – grabbing onto my keys, wallet and phone as well. It would have been far easier to deal with them one at a time, but I couldn't let go of either of them for long enough to do that. I felt like I was living inside the fox and duck puzzle where you have to get both animals and a bag of corn across a river in a boat that can only carry you and one other at a time. And you can't leave the fox with the duck or the duck with the corn! Mine was a simple task that parents carry out thousands of times without giving it a second thought, but it was taxing me to the extreme.

As we left our street, I put my hand on the passenger seat beside me, as though connecting with the hand I used to hold so often. I think Harry noticed from his car seat behind me. He asked, 'Who sits there, Daddy?'

'Oh Harry.' I sighed deeply, exhaling all the air from my lungs before diving in. 'That was Mummy's seat, wasn't it? That's where Mummy sat when we went in the car together, but she can't sit there any more, can she?'

'Why not, Daddy? I want her to.'

I had to force back a tear and wondered if I was saying the right things. I couldn't blank Mummy out, nor could I pretend she hadn't died. 'Mummy's in heaven now, with God and the angels. We miss her, don't we?'

'Yes, Daddy.'

I looked at Harry in the rear view, and a deadpan face looked back. He didn't understand, but he had the look of a boy far wiser than his years; a boy who has had to grow up too fast, in too short a time.

En route, I was confronted with the same fox-and-duck task when Emily needed changing and Harry needed the loo. I stopped at a service station, but was faced with a dilemma: men's loos don't have a baby room, I couldn't go into the ladies' and no dedicated baby changing room had a loo, as I remembered from Harry's nappy days. As I went into the building, a changing bag slung across one shoulder and Emily over the other, I started sweating from my rising anxiety. I was also holding Harry's hand tightly for fear of losing him. Emily was crying and Harry was trying to pull away, so I held him tighter and made him cry as well. By the time – to my utter relief – I found a family baby changing room in which I could shut us all inside, I was shaking. When Harry wouldn't use the loo because its seat had the front cut away, I wanted to burst into tears. I changed Emily's filthy nappy and begged Harry to use the loo before he had an accident.

We made it back to the car and everyone was strapped in again. I set off, only then realising that I hadn't used the loo myself. Hell and damnation. I couldn't face running the same marathon again, so carried on in discomfort.

On our arrival in Wiltshire, Guy and his lovely wife, Annabel, who I met for the first time, welcomed me with open arms. I breathed for what felt like the first time, thankful that the journey was finally over. Making myself at home in their kitchen, I boiled a kettle, sterilised bottles and made up Emily's feeds to last through until the morning.

Harry was shy at first, but soon made friends with Guy and Annabel's son, William, and they spent the afternoon running naked through the garden, splashing around with a hose and paddling pool. I watched them from the sidelines, preferring to sit in the quiet of the shade with Emily.

Guy had, before we came down, asked whether I would prefer to have a quiet weekend, or if I would like them to invite some others to dinner. I had replied that I'd be happy with sociability, but as the evening drew nearer my bravado fell away. I've always been shy and found meeting new people difficult, but with Percy beside me it was never too hard. Love her, hate her (did anybody?) you couldn't miss Percy. Diminutive in stature but larger than life, she wasn't afraid to speak up or speak her mind. She had a vibrant sense of humour, a laugh that was infectious and a positive, often hopelessly romantic, view of the world. It made meeting and entertaining people together easy.

When Guy's neighbour and her boyfriend knocked on the door, I felt sick and my palms were clammy. Fear ran through me. Do they know? Will they ask? What will they say? What will they think when they look at me? I just wanted to be at home, the door locked against the world, with my music and memories to cry to.

In the event, as is so often the case, the anticipation was a thousand times worse than the reality. I felt they just took me as I was, acknowledged that I was a dad bottle-feeding his baby and got on with things. When I allowed myself to leave my world behind for a moment, it was a very entertaining evening and the laughter felt good, albeit briefly.

In the morning, with everybody washed, dressed and fed, we went in convoy with another family – friends of Guy and Annabel – to

Longleat. Lacking the courage to spoil the party, I went along with it, once again wishing I could just hide in the shadows. I have the photographs to remind me of what we did that morning and how Harry loved the parakeet display and the mini train ride, but what I remember most is playing mother, feeding Emily in my arms on a picnic bench, winding her and shielding her from the sun in her pram. I was trying so hard to be a father and a mother at the same time, trying to give both our children the love, support and confidence that they so deserved, but all the while I was struggling with my pain, and Harry's.

'The show must go on', I knew, but it was tearing me apart inside. The only thing that seemed to keep me functioning was the watch I bought after Jessica's death. I hadn't worn one in years, relying on my mobile for checking the time, but now timekeeping and routine – feed, sleep, change; feed, sleep, bath; feed, bed – gave a structure and purpose to the day, a reason for me to keep putting one foot in front of the other. 'Don't let the buggers grind you down,' I heard my grandfather's voice telling me, time and time again. They could take my wife from me, it felt like they'd taken my life from me, but somehow, anyhow, I wasn't going to be beaten. Jessica wouldn't have been, and nor would I.

If It Wasn't for the Nights

In the evenings, Ali would bath both Harry and Emily, then put Emily straight into her Moses basket. Some evenings Harry would go to bed at the same time as her, others he would stay up a little longer with me. And at half past six Ali would stop work, leaving us alone.

It was all very well having a nanny – I couldn't have coped without Ali and she was very easy to get along with, plus I was incredibly fortunate to be able (chiefly thanks to Granny) to afford her wages – but I hated it. I hated having someone around the house; hated someone else looking after my babies. Jessica and I had never had a nanny, partly because of the cost and partly because we were both hands-on parents. Indeed, we'd only ever used a babysitter on about six occasions since Harry had been born.

But I recognised that this was a necessary part of our new life. Much of the time I was barely able to look after myself (Ali frequently suggested I eat something or have a sleep) and I was permanently exhausted, to the point where if I sat down for more than five minutes I would, invariably, fall fast asleep.

At the weekends, everything was different; with Ali off, I was left to my own devices. I dreaded the weekends, but they were my time with Harry and Emily as Dad. Several times friends and family suggested getting other help to get me through them, even on an occasional basis, but I couldn't do it. I felt it would have been a cop-out – a dereliction of duty. So instead, we struggled through from Friday night to Monday morning, sometimes not getting any further than the corner shop to buy bread and milk, often not going anywhere at all.

Leaving the house was a logistical nightmare for me. I couldn't even go out for ten minutes without making sure that Harry had done a pee, Emily was changed, I had a spare nappy with me and that everyone had the right shoes and coats on. (Plus the one thing I still always forget – a tissue for drippy noses.) Every move had to be planned meticulously, with a contingency in place for any situation, helping me to cope with my anxiety.

Bath time was my nemesis. I would try to do everything properly, by the book: cleaning each of Emily's eyes with a separate piece of cotton wool and holding her securely in the crook of my elbow, while Harry splashed at the other end of the bath. But it was too much of a juggling act for me to keep both children safe in the water, then get them dry and changed, ready for bed. Increasingly, I found it easier to take shortcuts with Emily so that I could deal with Harry, chasing him around the bedroom or bathroom as required. All too often, I just washed her face and put her in her cot, focusing more on Harry. Even so, it wasn't easy to get through the whole routine with him without a fight.

In desperation once, having failed to tear Harry away from the television to go upstairs and get undressed, I brokered a deal. 'Harry,' I began, tentatively. 'We just need to get you bathed and ready for bed. If I get in the bath, will you get in with me?'

'What? In the bath? You and me?' He was incredulous. But curiosity got the better of him and, sure enough, he got in with me, his tantrums and tears suddenly giving way to screams of delight and laughter. 'Daddy, you're hairy! Daddy splash me! Daddy, can I splash you?'

Another battle in the long war was won, by cunning, stealth and ingenuity.

In the months after Jessica's death, Harry's bedtime routine evolved to include two prayers as I said goodnight to him. They are not fixed, never quite the same as the night before, and are custom-ised to reflect our mood and the level of pain we (or I) feel we can handle at the time. These are the core texts. Harry calls them his 'Amens'.

God bless Harry and Bear,
God bless Emily,
God bless Mummy in Heaven,
God bless Daddy,
God bless Gran and Grandpa, Granny Cat, Granny Min and Grandpa Tim.
God bless all of Harry and Emily's friends and family and everyone who loves them.
    Amen.

Dear God,
Thank you for looking after us last night and today and for all the lovely things we've done. Thank you for looking after Mummy in Heaven, and thank you, too, to the angels for looking after Mummy and keeping her safe for us. We know Mummy loves Harry and Emily and Daddy, and she is so proud of us. Please tell Mummy that we love her and miss her so much, and that we think about her and remember all the fun things we did with her; cooking, gardening, going for walks, playing in the park and building train tracks. Please God, ask the angels to keep Mummy

safe always, and look after us tonight as well, while we're asleep, and all
day tomorrow, and help us to have lots of fun.

Amen.

And with Laura's print of the photograph of Jessica now hanging high in Harry and Emily's bedroom, their mummy is still watching over them.

The evenings were hard. Once the children were both asleep, the house fell quiet and I'd be alone with my thoughts and emotions. I rarely turned on the television when I was on my own in the first year to eighteen months after Jessica's death. Instead I found comfort in wine.

I had drunk little in the first couple of weeks, but when I went out for supper with friends or they came over, I drank more and more. I wasn't interested in moderation. I drank because it numbed and I drank because it made me sleep. The worst part of the daily routine was my own bedtime. I couldn't bear the empty bedroom, and I loathed the quiet of the darkness, where my thoughts became intolerable.

I sat, always at the kitchen table, with music playing – songs that reminded me of Jessica and songs that struck a chord with me. So much music, be it pop, rock, indie, is about love, unrequited and broken, and this provided me with an endless source of lyrics to which I could relate. And all the while I drank. I'd remember to eat at some point in the evening – a delivered pizza or Indian, ready-meals from the supermarket, a shepherd's pie that someone had kindly thought to drop off – and there I would sit, night after night.

I started smoking again in that first August. I had given up, eighteen months previously, after going to the funeral of the builder who had put in our new kitchen. He'd died of throat cancer about six months after he'd finished working for us. I'd been so moved by the grown men and his sons crying at the service that I had quit smoking the next day, not wanting to put Harry through the same ordeal.

But now that Jessica was dead it was different. I cared little for my own health and well-being and was finding that conversations with friends and family now triggered the same need for a stress-busting fag that I had felt for so much of my adult life as a smoker, so I caved in. (I didn't – wouldn't – smoke in the house and always went out into the garden to smoke, sitting on the bench or standing on the step down from the terrace to the grass; I also never smoked within an hour of needing to go near Emily.)

Fuelled by the alcohol, the evocative music and my own emotions and thoughts, I would cry in the garden, looking up at the night sky and when the tears burned dry into my face I would cry out and scream: 'Why us? Why Jessica? What did we do to deserve this?' It was so often hard to find the space and privacy to cry, but the darkness of garden, after the neighbours had turned out their lights and gone to bed, was mine.

My lifelines on these long, lonely evenings were the telephone and the Internet. I began to use email for keeping in touch with people far more than I ever had before (it had always just been a business tool in the past) and spent many hours on the telephone.

My most frequent telephone companion was Marian. She and I had always got on well. I remember how Jessica and I would often sit up late with her when we went to stay for the weekend. We would talk, the three of us, long into the night, solving the problems of the world, laughing and making plans for the future.

Now I would speak to Marian on the phone for two or more hours at a time, tears and wine flowing at both ends of the line with pauses to 'put the cat out' – refill a glass or light a cigarette. We would often talk through what had happened, what the latest news from Claire was or where the case might lead. On more than one occasion I'd wake up in the morning with no recollection of the details of the previous evening's conversation, but they were always honest and frank talks. There was none of the skirting around the issue I experienced with so many other people who were frightened of upsetting me or fearful of saying the wrong thing. Marian would just say it like it was and that, in itself, was a comfort.

'I still can't believe she's dead,' she would say. 'What are you feeling at the moment, Ben? Are you coping? What's the hardest part? How can we make things just a little bit easier for you?' Marian was not afraid of asking hard questions; I appreciated that. And even if trying to answer them sometimes had me welling up inside or made my voice shaky and croaky, it meant that I was still talking about Jessica with someone.

Jessica was all I thought of and most of the time – other than when I talked about missing her with Harry, or sometimes in those late-night phone calls – my thoughts were locked away inside me, with nobody to share them. The world had become a very lonely and scary place.

By the time I felt able to crawl up to bed it would frequently be one or two o'clock in the morning (a far cry from watching the nightly news headlines in bed and falling asleep with a book on my face) and I would have got through two bottles of white wine. Then sleep came easier, assuming, of course, I hadn't fallen asleep earlier at the kitchen table.

Although I was under no illusions about the foolishness of getting into a car (not that I could, with Harry and Emily asleep upstairs), I never felt I was so drunk as to be unable to attend to the children. With Emily needing to be changed and then have a feed between eleven and midnight for at least the first six months, I was getting used to the night shift. Harry would often wake as well, sometimes having heard Emily's cries, sometimes because he'd wet his bed. Even with pull-on nappies, the sheets were often soaked, so at any time in the night I would find myself comforting and changing him, then stripping the bed. Once or twice he was sick in the night – a tummy bug, or too much chocolate cake at a tea party – and I'd be glad of the wine to help me through the unenviable task of removing chunks from the bed and off the floor, before changing the sheets, his pyjamas and, more than once, washing the sick out of his hair.

And, despite the wine, I was alert throughout the night to the slightest cry, my 'mother's ear' always listening. Emily slept in her Moses basket at the foot of my bed and Harry was directly opposite, across the small upstairs landing. If Harry woke and couldn't sleep he would climb into bed beside me and we'd cuddle up. Then I could hear both of my children breathing and it felt safe, the three of us within arms' reach of one another.

In the mornings I'd get milk, tea and formula ready in a finely choreographed dance of kettle boiling, powder scooping and microwaving, ensuring that each of us got the right drink, at the right temperature in the shortest possible time.

And another day would begin.

Nativity

At the end of November, Harry's nursery put on a nativity play. It was a mixture of nursery rhymes, Father Christmas and delivering letters as I remember, with Harry as one of the three little pigs. Ali and her boyfriend, Neil, had made him a foam piggy nose and tail and we borrowed a pink T-shirt and leggings from a friend.

I arrived for the show, alone and on the early side, and paid my pound towards a children's charity in exchange for a programme. I sat down, halfway from the back of the room, on the left-hand side, against the wall. I felt nervous – anxious even – and tried not to be noticed. Just as I did when I dropped Harry off or picked him up from nursery if Ali was on holiday or off work for the day. It always felt wrong to be lining up with all the other mothers. This was Jessica's world and I felt I was intruding.

I was also terrified of somebody saying, 'Is your wife ill today?' or 'Are you helping your wife out?' or 'It's so good to see a dad getting involved.' The silly thing is that the mums I knew (and most of the others), were well aware of What, Why and When and nobody *has* ever asked anything quite like that, but I still live in fear of it. It just means that I've then got to say something that is going to make the other person feel embarrassed or uncomfortable and I don't like doing that. Worse than any awkward questions though would have been kindness in any shape or form. My chin would have wobbled, my voice would have cracked and I wouldn't have been able to speak for tears. And men don't do that.

As the nursery filled up with parents, cameras and video recorders I shrank deeper and deeper into my seat. Two parents I didn't recognise came and sat in the same row as me, but left a spare seat between them and me. An understandable mistake with only good intent, but it cut through me like a knife. I wanted to jump up, scream and run out of the building, but I couldn't do that to Harry, so I sat, waiting for the play to start.

For most of the half-hour-long performance Harry sat (or was lying) in his house of sticks, but he came out, did his routine and delivered his line, to perfection. It was a great step up from the year before when Jessica and I had proudly sat together watching him, as a lantern bearer, process in with the other little ones and sit down at the side. It had been a brief appearance, but Jessica had squeezed my arm with pride, looking first at Harry then to me, to make sure I hadn't missed him. Now he was centre stage and I hated it all.

At the end, after rapturous applause, Mrs B stood up to make an announcement. 'Thank you to all the mummies and daddies for coming to watch our little play and we hope you'll all stay for a glass of mulled wine and a mince pie. There's one other thing, too: we have a prize draw for a bottle of wine. Please look on the back of your programmes and if you've got a gold star, you're our winner.' There was a loud rustling as everyone picked up their programmes and after a moment I turned over mine, just for the sake of it. And there it was. The gold star. Oh no, I thought. Not me. I really do not want to draw attention to myself.

Just then, Harry came and found me in the audience. I hugged and congratulated him but he was evasive and fidgety. Poor Harry had wet himself, lying on the floor of his house and his clothes were soaked. He didn't want any attention either, so we shared a mince pie and then slipped away.

The First Christmas

Christmas 2004 was looming. I was dreading it, and dreaded hearing yet another person telling me that it was something to look forward to, or that at least the children could have a nice time. Yes, I was going to somehow make it a nice Christmas for Harry and Emily, but how could any of us really be happy? Their mother and my wife was dead, and this would be no more apparent than at Christmas. I was angry, and my heart ached with a hollow deepness.

I saw Sally a lot, usually over coffee in Putney, sometimes watching the river flow by, after she'd dropped her children at Hurlingham School. I had really only known her well enough to say 'Hi' if I saw her at a Coys auction until a few months before Emily was born when I had gone with Coys (Chris, Sally and the rest of the company) to help out with their computers at an auction in Monaco. The friendship that had grown out of waiting at the airport and choosing presents for our sons together had strengthened and was now a valuable comfort to me.

Sally helped with advice on three-year-olds and babies, talked to me about school coffee mornings, and told me of children who had lost their mother at a tender age, and gone on to grow up happy and secure. She spoke from first-hand experience.

One morning in early December, as we sat drinking our coffees, Sally asked me if I'd done my Christmas shopping. I hadn't even given it a thought and answered vacantly, 'No. I don't know . . . I'll . . . I don't know. Maybe I'll do it on the Web.' The last thing I wanted to do was go Christmas shopping.

'You need to get some nice things for the children, Ben. Spoil them a bit. Why don't we go shopping together. How about Oxford Street?' Aargh, no way. There wasn't a chance in hell of my going up there and I told her so. 'How about Wimbledon then, Ben?' Again, that was too far and too unfamiliar.

'How about here in Putney? There are a couple of toy shops here,' I suggested. Putney was home territory for me and I couldn't – wouldn't – go further afield, without even really knowing why.

'What will you buy them?' Sally asked.

'I don't know. I can't think.' Too many questions and not enough answers. I didn't want to do any of this – all I wanted was for Percy to come home with a big smile and to tell me what she'd bought and how we could afford it all really, couldn't we?

Sally understood and made a plan for me despite my flustering. We shopped in Putney a week later and I came away with bags and bags of presents, plus a blue bicycle for Harry with a box on the back for carrying Bear.

'Ben, you shop like a bloke. It's no fun,' Sally complained, halfway through our expedition. 'Don't you want to compare everything in different shops?'

But I didn't want to. Yes, I am a bloke, but that was only part of the reason; it was also that I wanted to get the whole thing done and over as quickly as possible. I had been out for more than long enough already and wanted to get back to the safety of school or the house.

I had had several offers of places to go to spend Christmas, but didn't feel like taking any up, until one came from my paternal grandmother, Granny, or GG (Great Granny) to her numerous great-grandchildren. The invitation came via my mother, who relayed that Granny knew how hard it would be for me, and that as she was now ninety and had only recently been widowed for the third time, she would equally appreciate a quiet, low-key Christmas. Hesitant at first, I knew it made sense. We'd be doing each other a favour.

The first time Granny was widowed (in the Second World War) she was just 26 and had had four children (the first of whom had died within her first year). My father was the youngest. Like him, Granny never knew her own father. He was killed in the First World War before she had been born. So, despite her telling me how she couldn't imagine how my situation was, she came pretty close, having experienced both early bereavement and growing up without a parent.

My maternal grandfather who died in his early eighties when I was eighteen, might also have had an inkling about how I was feeling. He too had lost his first wife who died, far too young, from a brain tumour. Although they didn't have children, I have no doubt that he would have been full of understanding and wisdom had he been around now.

Granny helped me a lot financially, in particular with childcare, saying how grateful she had been that at least she hadn't had the burden of money worries when she was widowed with young children, and how I too could do without them.

We arrived at Granny's in the afternoon of Christmas Eve, in a car laden with all the usual paraphernalia plus presents for the children, including the bicycle for Harry hidden under some blankets.

I was in a nervous sweat, not least because I had never stayed a night in this house, although I knew it well enough having spent, throughout my life, many a day here, exploring its nooks and crannies. But I was also worried because it was bitterly cold and the central heating there was virtually non-existent. Granny had thoughtfully put an electric heater in the room I would be sharing with Emily, so she wouldn't be cold. Harry's was an adjoining room, and we would share the bathroom next door.

Granny's is a comfortable and well-worn house with a gravel driveway at the top of a hill that has seen many generations of children. And it ticks. My step-grandfather, who'd brought up my father from the age of seven, was a serious clock collector, so there were grandfather, grandmother and bracket clocks everywhere, tick-tocking away. There is also, above this sound, an eerie hush. I have always thought that if ever there was a haunted house, this would be it, particularly the long, dark corridor which leads past the bedrooms to the now dilapidated nursery, still full of toys that my father and his half-brothers once played with.

The morning room at the side of the hall has a large log fire and is the most used room. In my childhood my step-grandfather, who was paralysed down one side following a stroke, would sit to the left of the fireplace, reading *The Times*, doing crosswords and watching us play on the floor. Granny sat opposite on a two-seater sofa that was always crowded with grandchildren and her dogs. She was a great teacher of 'Patience' and we learnt many variations of the card game with her.

The house was also the place to go to play the newest electronic game. In the early 80s these weren't anything like as sophisticated as today's, but we loved playing 'Simon' and an early Atari-style tennis game on the television.

I put Emily in her bouncy chair on the rug, with an activity bar strapped in front of her and helped Harry to pull out the basket of buses, taxis and cars. He soon had an almighty traffic jam snaked around the room. Granny's latest dog, Jet – a rescue dog of indeterminate age – was, although used to children, quite perturbed at being driven over by a double-decker.

After the children's tea I unpacked their clothes and ran a bath for them, getting them in and out as quickly as possible before they got too cold. Then, with a beaker of warm milk for Harry and a bottle of formula for Emily I had them ready for bed. After reading Harry a story I went downstairs, tired and aching.

Granny helped me to unload the parcels from the car and arrange them in her upstairs drawing room. I don't think I had ever been in here before; it is a much more formal and ornate room than the one below. Granny had asked my uncle to place a magnificent Christmas tree in the window, covered in bright baubles and lights. She was going to make sure it was a wonderful Christmas for Harry and Emily, and I had no doubt that she was going to do her best for me, but in a very low-key and unfussy way.

Then Granny went off to have a bath so I went downstairs and stepped out of the back door into the garden for a cigarette. Already the frost was settling, and in the clear and starry night I could see the garden stretching away from the house. As I smoked I could see the fish pond in the moonlight with rose beds around it. The gardener had, at Granny's request, built a fence around it to stop Harry falling in. You angel, Granny, I thought. The tall trees cast shadows on the sparkling lawns. How could this world be at once so hostile and yet so magical?

When I went back inside to the fireplace, Granny was downstairs again and had prepared a drinks tray. 'Would you like a gin and tonic? Would you make one for me? I don't drink when I'm alone, but I dare say we can treat ourselves.' There was ice, lemon and a bowl of crisps. So while I prepared two drinks, Granny went on to clarify her concept of drinking alone: apparently drinking a glass of wine while talking to someone on the telephone who also has one does not constitute drinking 'alone'. I love Granny – she's a diamond.

Despite having drawn an unfairly large proportion of short straws she can only see the good in life.

When we sat down, Granny told me that we were going to talk openly and honestly, as we were now both 'In the Club'. She never once complained about her life, or allowed me any self-pity, but we talked about all the highs and lows of life and she confided in me in a way that made me feel important, loved and not as alone as I wanted to believe.

So many people have judged me, not in the sense of what I have or haven't done, but by deciding, with no way of knowing the truth, where I 'am'. People always draw on their own experiences to try and second-guess what is going on in my head and how I am feeling. We all suffer in some way at one stage or another in our lives, but losing a wife and mother days after childbirth, and being left not only with a broken heart, but with a confused three-year-old and a newborn baby who is needy and demanding, is not the same as losing a grandparent, a parent, or a friend.

Statistically I was in a minority – it is much more common for a man to die, leaving a young family – and finding someone who understood how I really felt was hard, especially when it came to the despair and guilt at being the one who was still here to enjoy the triumphs of baby's first smile, first laugh and first steps.

Granny showed me, in simple terms and without judging me, or my life, that she was aware of all of this and that I should allow people to not understand.

We bonded in our 'club'.

In the morning, Harry woke me early. 'Daddy, Daddy, guess who's been in the night?'

'I don't know, Harry. What's happened?' I played along, trying to build his excitement.

'Father Christmas, Daddy, and look what he's brought me!'

Harry had already emptied his stocking and dumped an armful of goodies on my bed. 'Emily, look!' he went on. 'Emily, Father Christmas brought you some presents. Daddy, look, Emily's got some presents too.'

Harry's excitement was contagious and together we helped Emily to unpack her slightly smaller stocking. If only Percy could see them now. If only she could share in the joy of Emily's first Christmas. I blinked away my tears, determined that my own misery and deep, deep pain would not spoil the day for the children. They saw me cry often, but I didn't want them to on Christmas Day – not if I could help it. I had to give them the chance to enjoy the day and forget our troubles.

The four of us drove to Granny's village church for the mid-morning service and, as we took a pew towards the back, Granny proudly introduced us to people she knew. 'This is my grandson and these are my great-grandchildren,' and all the while I was thinking, Please, don't anybody say anything kind or inquisitive – I won't be able to cope.

I've never been confirmed, although with a Catholic upbringing I received First Communion and would, if I visited the confessional, be able to take communion in a Catholic church. Jessica and I had chosen to bring Harry up in the Church of England and when she went to take communion, Harry and I would join her for a blessing.

When I took the children up to the altar rail with Granny, the vicar, who had throughout the service been wearing a flashing reindeer hairband, looked at us. Emily's face screwed up in horror as I held her forward for her blessing. The hair on the back of my neck prickled and I started to break out in a cold sweat. People were looking at us, weren't they? Maybe, maybe not, but I felt terribly uncomfortable and panicky and we fled back to the safety of the pew as fast as I could guide Harry.

It was a welcome moment for me when we left the church, via the icy path, and drove back up the hill to Granny's house for turkey and mass unwrapping of presents.

There's a tradition in our family that we always have a Christmas Tree Party. It always takes place at Temple, my aunt and uncle's house, so on Boxing Day I drove over there with Granny, Harry and Emily at tea time. The children usually all sit down for tea in the kitchen while the grown-ups sit in the next-door dining room, watching with amusement through a butler's hatch. I stayed in the kitchen with Harry and Emily, offering them sandwiches, crisps and biscuits. And as I sat there I could see in my mind images of the previous Christmas: Jessica standing behind Harry – in much the same way as I was now – talking to Laura; moving the scrunchie from her wrist, to her hair and back again. And her laugh. It was ringing in my ears and all I wanted was to run home with the children and shut us away. I played on though – I had to for Harry; he was so excited.

The real moment that the children wait for comes after tea. They all sit cross-legged on the drawing room floor and John calls out each child's name, starting with the youngest. Then, either in their parents' arms, or as they get older, under their own steam, they go up and choose a small gift from the tree. The skill is not to choose a decoration, but one of the many cars, crayons, purses or whoopee cushions that have been taped onto the branches.

I sat on the floor with Emily clasped on my lap, and Harry for the most part sitting next to and against me – all huddled up together for safety. I studiously ignored most of the room, preferring to go unnoticed, and other than Mum, I only allowed Granny to hold Emily. She had passed the test over the last few days and I didn't worry about letting Emily go to Granny for a cuddle. Nevertheless, I hovered near by.

I was terrified of anything that anybody might say. It was six months since Jessica had died and I was already being told by people that I 'should be moving on now' or that they 'expect things are getting easier for you, aren't they?'

How little people understood. How often people assuage their own fears and anxieties by telling you how *you* must be all right by now, with little or no regard for the reality. Why does no one ask rather than tell? The truth is, as I learnt from a handout from a bereavement course that Laura attended as part of her medical training, that it is a typical six-month scenario: everybody else has forgotten about the funeral, is getting on with their own life and barely gives a thought to the deceased or their family. Also typical, is that for the bereaved husband or wife, it takes about six months for the shock to wear off and for the complete awfulness of the situation to sink in, finally – just as the help, support and concern begin to dry up, leaving one very, very alone, isolated and frightened. When Laura had shown me the handout, which took the form of a timeline, I instantly recognised the terrible roller coaster of emotions in the early stages, then baulked at the very long way I still had to go.

In the end, there were no major foot-in-mouth comments and I was just accepted and made part of the party this time. Still, I was glad to get to Burhunt, just up the road, and to shut out the world. But hard as I tried I couldn't relax, even in the house I grew up in. All I wanted was to be at home, in our house – Jessica's, Harry's, Emily's and my house.

Jessica's Tree

During that first autumn term in 2004, Mrs B had sent a letter home from nursery to parents, explaining that she wanted to invite them to contribute towards the cost of planting a tree in Wimbledon Park, in Jessica's memory. I was so touched when she first mentioned it to me. How perfect for the children. Jessica had spent many hours in the park with Harry – and me at weekends – walking, playing on the swings and feeding the ducks on the pond. It is just a short walk from our house and the children were both spending a lot of time there with Ali.

The council had over-ordered trees and said that there was a large magnolia to spare. They would be happy to find a good place for it rather than return it to the grower. We would also be allowed to put a plaque in front of it, so long as it followed their guidelines. So I started the fund off with a twenty, and hoped there'd be enough money collected to pay for both tree and plaque.

In January, a time was fixed with the council to plant the tree. Emily and I met up with Mrs B, Emma, Harry and three of his friends in the park. It was a charity fundraising day, so the children were dressed in their pyjamas inside their boots and coats. Harry held Bear close to him as well. 'Did you see the diggers, Daddy?' he cried. His excitement was palpable: he was on an out-of-school trip *and* he'd seen the diggers at work.

A hole had already been excavated for the tree, which was huge – at least fifteen feet tall and with an enormous root ball. So when the children were ready and watching, six men lifted and dragged the tree into the hole, and we aligned it with its best view facing down the path. First Harry and then his friends had a go at shovelling the heavy clay soil into the hole, but it was hard work. They soon lost interest and turned their attention instead to the digger, and, with the foreman's permission, scrambled into it eagerly.

The significance of planting Mummy's Tree was largely lost on the children, but Harry's chest had been puffed out, bursting with pride. This was an adventure and a treat, and it was for Mummy. It made her real again to him, and meant that his friends knew that he'd had a mother just like they did, even if she was no longer alive.

To have had a mother was and is important to Harry; it makes him fit in with his friends. He hates being different.

Emily's Christening

On the first weekend in February 2005 Emily was christened.

I'd thought long and hard about godparents and deliberately chose friends and family of Jessica's – Nick, with whom she and Phil and grown up, and her two first cousins, Alice and Alexandra. Jessica was Alice's godmother as well. I wanted to show that, even though I had withdrawn into myself, I wasn't cutting them out. It was a political decision, but I also felt it was right for Emily to have an influence in her life that stemmed from the mother she would never know.

I dressed Emily in the same christening gown that Harry had worn – a beautiful and much-handed down gown from my maternal grandmother, Gar's, family. Emily only just squeezed into the dress, which had been designed for younger, smaller babies than she had been, even at birth. When Jessica had held Harry in the gown, it had come down past her knees. Now I held Emily tightly, determined to get through the day with a strength that I could barely muster, thinking all the while how it should have been.

Emily beamed at April as she held her above the font, and Harry played on the steps around it in the blue coat Jessica had bought for him the previous winter – big enough to last two seasons. I stood to the side, wearing a jacket and tie and shirt, the collar of which was too tight and itched. Despite the cold chill in the air I was sweating and my forehead prickled. Rather than a smile I wore a grimace; all I could see was Jessica's coffin at the front of the church and all I could think of was how cold the grave outside must be.

In her prayers April mentioned 'those that have died, including Emily's mother, Jessica', and when I carried Emily up to the altar, making my way through the congregation and choir, I felt happier that the absence of a mother had been explained. I doubt it was necessary – I'm sure everyone there knew why there were only three of us – but it also made the service so much more poignant.

Afterwards, we posed outside the South Door for the obligatory photographs – godfather and two godmothers, Emily and I, just as we had three years before at Harry's christening. But by now I'd had more than enough of drawing similarities.

With our extended families, we drove the short way back to Burhunt for lunch, where, in a tense and slightly diffident way, I held it together, although I was shaking inside. As Christine left she told me what a good day it had been and how well it had gone. And, after everyone else had gone, I broke down in tears and sobbed. What had been good about it? The day had been an impossible ordeal, carried out only for others' benefit. Could nobody understand or imagine my pain?

After the children's tea I went back to the graveyard in the dark and sat against the wall behind Jessica's grave, sobbing at the mound of earth, begging her to tell me why she had left us. At times I hated Jessica for leaving, for forcing me to be both widower and single parent. It's crazy to think of it like that, but in a world of madness it made as much sense as anything else. I just kept thinking that if she'd really, really tried she could have hung on that little bit longer to let the drugs do their work. Couldn't she?

In June, Harry, Emily and I returned to Wimbledon Park to position the plaque at the tree's base with another group of friends from nursery. It was a considerably warmer day this time and the tree was growing well and strong and was covered in thick green leaves. Harry stood next to Emily's pushchair, watching as the hole for the concrete was dug. He clutched Bear under one arm and held up the small black sign by its foot-long spike. It read, '*Magnoliaceae. Magnolia x loebneri* "Merrill". Arboretum origin.' Including the botanical information was what enabled us to have a plaque in front of the tree, but all we really wanted to see was inscribed underneath: 'Jessica's tree. 22nd May 1970–30th June 2004'. Which said it all.

Harry's five friends stood in a solemn line to his right and together they watched the earth being dug out and the concrete and water being poured in. Then, with the official business over, Mrs B bought a round of ice creams and we sat in the shade of a tree to eat them. Emily, almost a year old now, wore most of her ice cream all over her face, down her T-shirt and across her legs. She didn't care though – she was having far too much fun. Jessica would have had wet wipes with her to clean her baby's face, but I only had a rather crumpled piece of tissue.

One day I'll get it right, I thought.

A New Nanny

Ali gave her notice in late February 2005. It wasn't an easy decision for her, but she wanted to go back to Australia for the trial of her sister's murder, and while it didn't come as a total surprise, it nevertheless sent me into a panic. What would I do? How would I find another nanny?

After the initial shock, I got in touch with a nanny agency in Fulham that Jessica had used to find a doula-like maternity nurse when Harry was born and it felt right to go back to them now. We had been persuaded by our parents to have experienced help during the night when Harry was a newborn so that Jessica could sleep, but afterwards, although she had been full of good advice, we felt it hadn't been entirely necessary. Harry was a big strong boy and easily settled into a routine. So, having seen what a capable mother Jessica was, it never occurred to any of us to book someone for after the second pregnancy.

The agency snapped into action, firing CVs at me by email. I waded through them, putting those that didn't stand out to one side, and flagging some up for interviews. I met a steady stream of girls, always after the children's bedtime or when they were out during the day. I didn't want the change of nanny to be distressing for them and thought that a long line of possibles would only confuse them, Harry in particular.

I told Harry that Ali needed to go home to Australia, and we got out a children's atlas to see how far away that was. The other side of the world – what does that mean to a three-year-old? It was only a foot away in the book. So I explained to him, 'If you flew there in an aeroplane, like we did when we went on holiday with Mummy, it would take all day and all night to get there.'

Harry's eyes were wide open with wonder at this piece of information. 'What? So you'd have to have a bath in the aeroplane and sleep in it too? Where would you go to the loo?' Possibly, the scale of the distance was sinking in, and we agreed that it would be hard for Ali to come to work in the morning and get home for the night if she lived so far away.

'But I don't want another nanny, Daddy, 'cos I won't know her name.' He was genuinely perturbed and on the verge of tears with worry.

'Don't worry, Harry.' I sat him on my knee and cuddled him. 'When we find a really, really nice nanny Daddy will tell you her name before you meet her, and I promise that you'll like her as much as Ali. We'll find a nanny who's really good at playing.' Once satisfied that Daddy wouldn't leave him and Emily with a total stranger, without a proper introduction, Harry set about planning the games that they'd play together.

Interviewing people for a job was very strange. I had never done it before, as when I'd first met Ali it had just been for an informal chat. I was horribly nervous and, to start with, more worried about whether we were suitable for them than the other way round.

The agency had briefed all of the applicants on our circumstances, explaining that I was often at home during the day and that it would be a shared-care arrangement. Most nannies like sole care during their working hours, which I totally understood, but I didn't want to find myself shut out of domestic arrangements, meal planning and interactive play just because it was between eight in the morning and six in the evening. If Jessica had been here I would have been involved – she'd always made quite sure that I pulled my weight – and why should the children lose me as well during the week? Some nannies were put off by this, but others didn't seem to mind and one or two of them seemed especially warm, friendly and capable, so I asked them back to meet Harry and Emily, and to see how the three interacted.

One girl, another Australian, seemed perfect, but when I rang the agency the following day to say that I was seriously considering offering her the job, I was told 'I'm sorry, she's no longer interested in the position.'

Apparently it was the shared-care issue again. Damnation. This was going to be harder than I'd realised, although on reflection it was probably a good thing as she was too pretty and I was terrified of things getting complicated. The NCT mums had said to me, 'All we have to do now is find you a pretty nanny to fall in love with,' and only half serious though it was, I'd hated the idea. I didn't want to fall in love.

Having run out of suitable candidates – none was 'just right', although in another life, or with children of a different age, I would have employed several of them – I returned to an email from Katie, one of the mothers at nursery, that I had skipped over and not followed up.

Katie worked part time for another agency in Wimbledon. I talked to her at length about what I was looking for in a nanny, and she very quickly followed up, emailing me with six CVs and her summary of the candidates.

Again, I filtered through CVs and one or two dropped out immediately because of the sole-charge issue. Both Katie and Lucy at the agency were now working hard to find me the best nanny they could, but I was starting to feel despondent – time was running out.

In an email over Easter, Katie pressed me to consider interviewing a girl called Carly whom she had met. I had put her CV to the bottom of the pile because she was so young and I didn't believe she would be able to give Harry and Emily what they needed. I'd also half thought that Katie was pushing her forward just because it was she who had originally signed her up to the agency. I went on meeting other candidates, some of whom I liked, but took alternative jobs. It seemed as though I was going round in circles and would never find someone who was just right.

So, with no more CVs to look at and having drawn a complete blank, I changed my mind and agreed to interview Carly. I was immediately impressed with her calm disposition and a maturity beyond her years. Also, her boyfriend had two daughters whose mother had died only about six months before Jessica. The girls were older than Harry and Emily, but Carly was full of good ideas about how to celebrate mothers' birthdays and keep their memory alive.

A few days later, she came for a second interview, this time with Harry, Emily and Ali. I left them to it, just looking in on them once or twice as they played on the sitting-room floor.

They all raved about Carly. 'She'd be perfect, Ben. She's really, really nice,' Ali said after she had gone.

If she'd have us, I was now certain we'd found another Mary Poppins. Why on earth had I resisted meeting her for so long, just because of her age? I will never again judge a book by its cover.

Carly started three weeks later, working alongside Ali on the Friday for a day's handover. In the evening Ali said again, 'You've made a good choice, Ben. She's perfect for the children.' We all knew so.

Jessica's Birthday

Jessica's birthday was on the 22nd May 2005. She would have been 35.

To mark the day, I went to the party shop where we'd gone in the past to organise tables and chairs for Harry's birthday parties in the garden, and bought a large helium balloon with a picture of a birthday cake on both sides. I took the balloon home to the children and we sat together on the sofa where, using a big, thick black felt pen, I wrote around the balloon's edge: 'To Mummy, we love you from Emily and Daddy XX.' Harry then wrote his own name and two kisses above Emily's and mine. Emily also had a go at making a mark with the pen but preferred to sit in her white-and-pink bear-face babygro on the sofa, and just point at the balloon. It was exciting for her and she had no concept of the balloon's significance.

Then, dressed up in fleece jackets, we went out into the garden, Harry glowing with pride as he stood on the grass, holding the balloon to his cheek.

'One – two – three – go!' we said together, and he let go. The balloon rose up, before being caught by the wind and carried gently away, higher and higher, over the roof of our house, rising up to Mummy in heaven. Harry was excited by its ascent, providing a running commentary of its progress.

I gave each of the children a memory book when we went back inside. I'd been working on them for a few weeks. Sally and I had made lists of different ideas for inclusion, so that each had – all laminated for protection against spills – pages of Mummy's favourite things, facts about Mummy ('Mummy was born on a FRIDAY; Mummy's star sign was GEMINI; Mummy had BROWN eyes; Mummy had a big SMILE; Mummy had small FEET; Mummy was very KIND; Mummy was very PRETTY; Mummy loves HARRY and EMILY') and wrappers from some of her favourite chocolate bars – Toblerone, Dairy Milk and Curly Wurly.

I put in a page called 'Mummy's happiest days' as well. It contained a wedding photograph and the first photographs of her with both Harry and Emily, cradled in her arms after their deliveries. One page simply had a small lock of her hair, from the envelope the funeral director had given me. This didn't need an explanation.

I put Harry to bed at seven, but he didn't settle and reappeared a couple of times. At 8.10 p.m. he came down complaining of a tummy ache 'from too much milk', even though I had only given him his normal beakerful.

'I want to sleep in your bed, Daddy,' he said.

'No, Harry,' I answered. 'Let's tuck you up in your own bed.'

Ever since Jessica had died, Harry had been sleeping in my bed. Sometimes he'd go to bed there and I'd carry him to his room when I went up, other times he would appear in the middle of the night and wake me saying he was frightened or missed Mummy. 'Climb in and snuggle down, Harry. Let's try and go to sleep,' I'd say to him, only half awake. There were also times when he'd just arrive and I'd wake to an arm in my face.

I still loved this closeness, but didn't think I should continue to encourage it, so I'd started trying to suggest he slept in his own bed, which didn't always go down very well.

Harry went to the bathroom and did a pee, but when he came out he was angry. 'I don't want a babysitter and I don't like Mummy any more.'

Hearing this, I started to cry. There was no babysitter tonight, and I didn't go out that often. And anyway, why was it Mummy's fault? What had she done?

We sat down on the landing and talked. For the first time, Harry voiced a connection between 'borning [sic] a baby' and Mummy's death. Was this idea of his from suggestion or by deduction, I wondered.

'Mummy didn't want to die, Harry. Mummy misses you,' I promised him.

'Why are you sad, Daddy?' We were both in tears now, as I tried to comfort him.

'Mummy was my wife. When a woman becomes a wife and a man becomes a husband it means they love each other very, very much, and I miss Mummy, too,' I said.

'Why do you look worried, Daddy?' he went on.

'I'm proud of you, and I love you, Harry. I'm not worried,' I followed the absolute truth with a lie. Surely it was a white lie though? He so needed to feel safe and secure.

After I'd eventually settled Harry, I went downstairs and collapsed, exhausted, at the kitchen table with a glass of wine, my head in my hands and tears streaming down. It had been a while since I'd really cried and it suddenly seemed easy again.

Half an hour later there were more tears and wails from Harry. He was beside himself with fear, insecurity and anger. Emily woke up as well, and started to cry.

'I miss my mummy,' he said. I perched on his bed and sat him on my lap, cuddling and comforting him. Then, 'Why did Mummy and you fight and Mummy went to live in another house?'

Where on earth did that come from? Someone must have explained divorce to him at some point, and he was confusing the two situations, so I explained death to him all over again.

'But why can't Mummy be dead and live in a house?'

This was emotional overload and I no longer felt equipped with the right answers. Instead, I just lay down beside Harry on his bed and held him, whispering reassurances, until he drifted off.

Letter to Harry and Emily, 1

Sunday, 22 May 2005

My darlings Harry and Emily,

I look at you both asleep in your beds at night as I tuck you up and kiss your cheeks. You sleep so soundly, Harry, in the knowledge that you are safe and loved. And you, Emily, in the belief that your world is complete. One day you will understand that it isn't. What do you think when I hold you up in front of Mummy's photograph and say, 'That's Mummy; she really, really loves you'?

I am tired. Months of our new life have taken everything from me, and I feel as though I have been to hell and most of the way back again. I so don't want to have to go there ever again. Tears are exhausting. Grief is physically exhausting, almost more than its emotional exhaustion. Just keeping our life ticking over under these circumstances takes every ounce of energy. Keeping other people's lives ticking over as well is sometimes asking the impossible, but I have no choice. You need me more than ever before, and equally, at the same time, you make my life meaningful. You are now my sole reason. I love you both more than anything on this earth. I will always give you my all, though sometimes that isn't enough. You already give me your all. I draw what strength I have from your needs and from your unquestioning love for me.

We have no future though, least not one that I can see. It is like I am floating up and down in a cold, harsh ocean with no landmark on the horizon, clutching you both to me, just riding the swell, waiting for the wind and tides to take us where they will. There is no past any more, either. All of the things Mummy and I did together and with you, Harry, are just distant memories, and there is no one to reflect on them or to remember detail with, no one to look back at triumphs and disasters with and say, 'Yes, we did that,' or 'It was hard, but we beat it together.' We can't even laugh and tease one another about arguments we had any more; there is only pain there for me now.

Our second wedding anniversary since Mummy's death is looming, and after the past month, reliving her death after a year, I am too worn out to think about it. I know though that it, and many more to come, will be a very hard day to get through. I just hope and pray that it will be a little bit easier each time. Then there'll be a little let-up; just Christmas to look forward to with dread.

'Where has Mummy gone?' I have asked myself and others countless times over the months since her death. How can so much vitality and enthusiasm for life just vanish? Day by day the answer is becoming clearer. Mummy as we knew her is gone, but she lives on in our hearts and our memories, and she still lives on so much in you both. You are both strong willed, bright eyed and so, so loving. Both so like your mummy.
Daddy xx

Investigation – Part Two

In mid-October 2004, Claire Fazan had written to me and sent a copy of a letter from the Coroner confirming that she would now be holding an Inquest. In her letter, Claire also told me that she had wasted no time in instructing Philip Havers QC who was undoubtedly, to her mind, the best man for the job. He had already acted in some of the highest-profile inquests of recent years where there had been a question of clinical negligence. I was overawed. My own personal tragedy seemed to be rippling into ever-growing circles. I felt sure now that justice for Jessica would be just around the corner, although Claire warned me that the Inquest was unlikely to be listed before spring 2005.

Claire also instructed three expert witnesses – a microbiologist, a GP and a midwife – to help review the case notes. During the first half of 2005, Claire worked tirelessly, collating Jessica's medical files, witness statements from the staff at Kingston and the community midwife, and the medical experts' opinions on them all. Things moved slowly though, and while I had been warned that this might be the case, the delays between letters from Claire were sometimes painfully long.

In mid-February, the experts' reports started to filter through to me. This was the moment I had been waiting for – finally I would have a medical opinion on whether Jessica's death could have, should have, been avoided. The first was from the microbiologist. His conclusion was that by the time of Jessica's readmission to hospital, the fatal outcome was probably inevitable as her illness had developed so rapidly. But, he said, on the balance of probability, had she received aggressive resuscitation and intravenous antibiotics at any point before 6 a.m. on 29 June, she would have survived (although quite probably also requiring a hysterectomy to remove the primary focus of infection, had treatment not begun before some time on the Sunday).

I went into complete meltdown, screaming with rage as I held the report in my shaking hand. The cut-off point was barely eight hours before she was rushed into Casualty. It had been so close. This might never have happened. Christ knows, enough people could have changed the course of events. There had been more than enough time to save her life, but none of those responsible *had done a thing*. Nobody had bothered to stop and think, This is a very sick woman who needs emergency treatment or she'll die.

I wept and wept, at the knowledge of how close we had been to carrying on with our normal, boringly average family life. That was all we had wanted.

In her accompanying letter Claire wrote, as she did in so many of her subsequent ones, an acknowledgement of how difficult it would be for me to read, and that I need only pick up the telephone to talk it through with her.

Through March and April the letters kept coming. As each expert reviewed the notes and witness statements, focusing on their own area of expertise, the opinion was consistent. 'Sub-standard care' came up again and again, in relation to so many aspects of Jessica's post-natal days. It was a catalogue of disasters. How could one woman have drawn so many short straws?

As the full and closely scrutinised picture came together, Claire set up a case conference for early June, at Philip Havers' chambers, at which we would all meet to go through the history in minute detail, testing and examining the case. The conference bundle of notes contained incident review forms, every clinical note from Jessica's two stays in hospital, twenty or more witness statements from medical staff and Jessica's post-mortem report. On Claire's advice, I couldn't put off reading this any longer, as it would be discussed both at the conference and the Inquest. Tears streamed down my face as I read what each of her organs had weighed and whether her left lung was heavier than her right. Jessica, who had been so anxious not to have a Caesarean, had died in front of me a year earlier, as one organ failed after another, and had then been cut to pieces.

My paperwork filled two large lever-arch files, which I lugged along in a rucksack to the afternoon conference. We sat around the table – which was covered with white ring binders, legal pads and half-empty cups of tea and a plate of biscuits in between – for some three hours. I'd been told that I could leave the room at any time I wished, but I stayed, going out only once for a cigarette.

I was pulling out all the stops to try and keep up with the legal and medical implications of the case and wanted to understand fully exactly what had happened. It made for very painful listening. There was universal agreement that Jessica's care had been sub-standard and at some points in our re-run of events, experts would shake their heads. Nobody could believe that this was what had really happened. Least of all me – and I was there.

At one point during the conference, the microbiologist, Professor Cartwright, was asked about how Jessica's condition, both physically and mentally, would have been between the Sunday and Monday while she was in bed at home. His answer cut me like a knife – he described physical symptoms that I recognised, but also said that she would have been feeling very frightened and experiencing some degree of paranoia. 'It's symptom of the Group A strep' toxins,' he said.

Percy had been ill, in pain, scared and paranoid, and I hadn't stopped to notice or recognise how desperate and unwell she was. We had argued and been unnecessarily terse with each other. Why hadn't anybody realised? Why hadn't I done something – anything – for her? What impression had I given her? What thoughts had she died with? My hands began shaking and I think some of the others must have noticed. Philip asked me if I wanted to have a break from the room and I slipped out for a cigarette before rejoining them.

At the end of the conference Claire, Philip and I sat around the table alone to talk about the Inquest. There was still no word on a date, but we were going to request that the Coroner sit with a jury. Philip explained to me that he saw a strong case for the verdict being returned as one of 'Natural causes contributed to by neglect' – a very strong verdict and the only alternative open to a Coroner other than 'Natural causes' in these circumstances. He told me that a seasoned Coroner would not return this verdict lightly, and may err on the side of caution, but that a jury listening to the evidence would be far more likely to. Of course they would, I thought, who wouldn't? As I left, Claire once again apologised for my having to sit through it all and thanked me for my input. 'I hope you'll go home and have a stiff drink,' she said. 'Have you got anyone to keep you company, Ben?'

I had arranged already to go out for a drink and dinner with Sally, so I assured Claire that I would have a drink or two and that I'd be able to unwind a bit.

I hailed a cab to take me back to Fulham. I was hot and totally drained, my head buzzing from the wealth of information and detail I'd listened to during the conference. I felt shattered. I was going to get drunk.

Sally and I sat in a Thai bar drinking cocktails and I summarised the events of the afternoon to her. She listened both from the point of view of an NHS Nurse Practitioner and of a mother, tears in her eyes.

'But what a job you're doing, Ben,' she told me. 'Good for you for standing up for Jessica and for doing this for your children. They will be so proud of you one day. It must be so hard. I just can't imagine.'

I hadn't really thought about it in those terms. I just kept going and going and would see it through until the bitter end. Nothing could be worse than what had already happened, and I owed it to Jessica to turn over every stone, and to our children – for a time, as they got older, when they would begin asking searching and angry questions.

Starting School

The new Hurlingham School building had been open for almost a year, and to me it was familiar territory. Even so, I had nervously joined a tour to show new parents around and had been to the drinks party at the end of the summer term. I felt awkward and ill at ease – maybe because on both occasions I had put a jacket and tie on, much to the amusement of the staff who were more accustomed to seeing me around the school in jeans and a T-shirt.

To Harry though, the school was big and strange. When I took him for a uniform fitting, he was shy, refusing to try on anything while Carolyne, the mum who runs the school uniform shop, was watching. So we tried on each item, one by one, standing behind a folding screen (and only because of the promise of being allowed to raid Carolyne's sweet tin once we were finished).

On Harry's first morning, in September 2005, I took the obligatory 'First Day at School' photographs of him on the doorstep. He looked so grown up in grey shorts, pale blue blazer, cap and tie, yet he was only just four. When I delivered him to his classroom he clung on to me. He was nervous of letting go and meeting his classmates and Mrs Patterson, his teacher, even though we'd already met most of them at a picnic three days earlier, and Charlie – one of the other NCT children – was also in his class.

I promised Harry that he'd be all right, that I would be around the building all day, and that I'd collect him at home time. We looked on as the other children said goodbye to their mothers, some bravely, some in tears. Then I passed him to Mrs Patterson and slipped away.

For most of the morning I felt sick. I knew that Harry would be absolutely fine, and if he wasn't – well they'd tell me wouldn't they? But all I could think of was Jessica sitting in the car outside on that first morning of nursery. I was so proud of Harry and of the boy he was turning into, but had no one to share it with. I ached.

For the first few weeks, I tried hard not to run into Harry at school. I thought it might make him upset and, in any case, it was important for him to have his own space. Inevitably, I was finally spotted. 'Hi, Daddy!' I heard, and saw Harry waving both arms at me through the bars of the gate between the main corridor, The Avenue, and the playground. His friends hung onto the bars too. 'Hi, Harry's daddy!' they chorused. There was little doubt now: Harry felt as safe at school as I did. It would have been hard not to as it is a homely, welcoming and very, very friendly school.

Inquest

In mid-November Claire started preparation in earnest for the Inquest, which had been set for Monday, 28 November 2005, with the option for it to continue into the following day. Even at that late stage, the Coroner's Officer had not been able to confirm which witnesses would be attending. We knew that the Senior House Officer, the community midwife and various midwives and consultants from Kingston would be called, but it was not certain whether Dr Williams, the GP from our surgery, would be attending as she had been on compassionate leave, and nobody seemed able to say whether or not she had returned to work.

The Coroner suggested that Dr Christie, who was from the same practice and who had referred Jessica to hospital for her re-admission, might be called in her place if necessary. But Claire made it quite clear that this would be unacceptable to us as 'the matters in respect of which they can each give evidence are different'. Delaying the hearing until Dr Williams was able to attend could have left us in trouble though – the three-year time limit for commencing civil proceedings would expire in June 2007, and we needed both the evidence from the Inquest and time to prepare a case fully.

We had also been hoping to persuade the Coroner to call a jury to hear the Inquest. We knew that if twelve members of the public heard the case they would be as outraged as I was and we would be a step closer to a verdict of 'Natural causes, contributed to by neglect'. I was dismayed when we heard that the Coroner could see no reason to call a jury, as she was only obliged to do so if there had been a systemic failure, rather than mistakes by individuals. The systemic failure that I thought I could see was the lack of communication between all the various parties, but I had to accept this decision. In any case, I was sure that the evidence would speak for itself.

Claire had written to the solicitor acting for Kingston Hospital and the community midwife, asking whether they would be prepared to make a contribution to the costs of Harry, Emily and I being represented at Inquest. We would have Philip Havers, Claire and an expert witness – most probably our microbiologist. The combined bill would be, depending on whether it was one or two days long, in the region of £12–15,000, including a sum for preparation time. The solicitors wrote to Claire to 'confirm that they would not agree to such a payment' and so, with my insurers agreeing to cover my third with an ex-gratia payment, I forwarded a cheque to Claire for the children's remaining two thirds.

Claire and I had also discussed publicity and press coverage at some considerable length. I was becoming more and more determined that other mothers and their families should benefit from our tragedy, and so we agreed with David Standard – Irwin Mitchell's Head of PR – to put out an embargoed press release on the Friday before the Inquest started. We also agreed to fax a copy of it to the Coroner 24 hours in advance, so that there were no nasty surprises for her on the Monday morning. As inquests are held in public court, it is possible that it would have been reported anyway, but I wanted to make sure it got as wide a coverage as possible in order to warn as many mothers as I could.

As the end of the week before the Inquest drew closer, Claire and I spent more and more time in email and telephone contact, and I became more and more anxious. I knew, broadly speaking, what to expect in terms of the proceedings but not the outcome. I knew what I believed and I knew that I wanted a verdict of 'contributed to by neglect' returned. I also wanted my, or rather Jessica's, day in court. On the Friday, with the press release approved and sent out on the wire, Claire made sure I had her BlackBerry email address, mobile telephone number and home number, saying that she would be at home all weekend – planning to do some gardening – and that I should call her if I had any worries. 'But do try and relax, Ben, and not to worry too much,' she said.

I shut myself away with Harry and Emily over the weekend – I don't think we went out of the house once. I read through statements, letters and the press release, talking to Jessica and reminding myself what we were doing and why. Many times I sat on the sofa with the children, hugging them tightly, crying quietly to myself. Harry noticed once, and asked why I was sad. 'I'm all right, Harry,' I told him. 'I'm just so proud of you both and I love you more than you can imagine.'

'Do you love me as high as the moon, Daddy?'

'Much, much further than that, and all the way back again, Harry.' We were alluding to one of Harry's favourite books, *Guess How Much I Love You*, which tells of a parent hare's love for his child. Harry and Emily needed double love from me, and I feared that my loving them to beyond the edge of space and back again would not be enough.

On Sunday afternoon the doorbell rang. I'd been snoozing on the sofa while Emily was napping upstairs and Harry played on the floor. I answered the door and saw a young woman standing in front of me wearing an overcoat.

'Good afternoon, are you Ben Palmer?'

'Yes, that's right.' I was caught off-guard by the use of my name – she obviously wasn't selling double glazing or a new kitchen.

'I'm really sorry to trouble you, and I may have the wrong address and the wrong Ben Palmer, but are you going to court tomorrow?'

'Who are you?' The penny had half dropped, but I still couldn't work out who she was, and why she was ringing my doorbell. Then she told me her name and the paper she was from. I really hadn't expected this and felt it was a big intrusion.

'Please, leave us alone today. We're just trying to have a quiet family weekend before tomorrow. I'm really happy to talk to you then, but please let me be alone with my children for now.'

When I closed the door, I was shaking. I rang Claire, dragging her away from her herbaceous border. She calmed me down, saying, 'Don't worry, Ben – I think they'll leave you alone now, but at least we know there's interest in your story. When you get near to the Coroner's Court in the morning, call me on the mobile and I'll come and meet you.'

In the morning I took a taxi to the Coroner's Court in Bagleys Lane and called Claire, as instructed.

'You should be all right,' she said, 'the press are here, but we've asked them to back off a bit until later. I'll come down and meet you though, anyway.'

I was greatly relieved to hear all this. We had told the media that I would read a statement after the Inquest was over, and that I was happy to speak to them, but that I had an enormous mountain to climb, and had to focus on the fact that I would be first to give evidence.

Claire met me in the ground-floor hallway of the building, which looked more like a Victorian factory than a court of law. I preceded her up the stairs to the second floor, passing a man in a suit as I went. I looked studiously down at the floor and continued up the stairs.

'Ben, this is David Standard from our Sheffield office,' Claire called.

'David, I'm so sorry,' I said. 'I thought you were press!'

I felt silly, but he immediately put me at ease, telling me not to worry, that he was there to help and support me. 'Think of me as your bodyguard,' he said, smiling, his hand on my shoulder.

Together, Claire and David took me up to the courtroom, past a hushed group from the NHS and an equally hushed group of the press. Some of my family and friends were also starting to gather.

The courtroom was not at all what I had expected. The way it was furnished made it look more like a doctor's waiting room than the court sets you see on TV dramas, although it did have a raised wooden bench and witness stand at the far end.

Claire showed me where everyone would be sitting. Beside one of the water glasses on the tables was a handy-pack of tissues. 'Those are for you, Ben,' Claire said.

There could be no pretence now, this was going to be a very harrowing day, and not only for me.

There had been a moment's worry when we read one of the morning papers' headlines: 'The medical blunders that cost a new mother's life'. We weren't at all sure how much the Coroner would like the use of the word 'blunder', but the article itself was an accurate version of the story, based on our press release and some additional background research. It also included the quotes that Claire and I had put at the end of the release: 'I am determined that no other family should have to live through a tragedy like the one we have suffered'; and from Claire, 'Had [Jessica] been kept in hospital or referred back earlier, it is probable that she would still be alive today. Her family need to know why this did not happen. We hope the Inquest will provide them with some answers.'

The word 'probable' always jarred with me, but a solicitor would have to use it. As a widower and single parent I didn't have to; I was certain that Jessica would have been alive. Claire knew it too.

By ten o'clock the courtroom was full. Philip Havers, the barrister who was acting for Dr Williams and the solicitor who was acting for both Kingston and St George's hospitals (for the community midwife) were in their places in the front row; Claire, Professor Cartwright and I were in the second row, with the jury box that wouldn't be used on our left; and Claire's legal assistant, Emily, was behind us. The upholstered seats behind her (the 'public gallery') were full – my family, Jessica's parents and some of our friends were there, as well as the other witnesses who would be called and a small, quiet lady from one of the NHS trusts, who sat at the very back. A number of reporters had also squeezed in.

'All rise, this court is now in session.' The Coroner's Officer called everyone's attention and the Coroner entered from a side door behind the bench. I put my hand into my jacket pocket and held Jessica's scrunchie, which I had put in there for moral support. I also had a photograph of her in my inside pocket, close to my heart.

This was Jessica's day and what I had to do, I did through my love for her.

Having outlined the case before her, the Coroner very soon called me to the witness box. Terrified, but somehow composed, I was determined to do my best. I refused a glass of water and made my oath on the Bible. The Coroner took me through my recollections of events, sometimes referring to my lengthy written statement, asking for clarification. As we got deeper and deeper into my memories, the room around me faded from my vision, along with most of the people in it. Once or twice I choked on my words – fighting back tears as vivid memories were forced in front of my mind's eye.

Other than reading through my statement, I hadn't prepared, and some of the details I was asked for were hard to recall. I tripped up at one point, muddling the readings I'd taken for Jessica's temperature and giving an incorrect answer to a question. The Coroner picked me up on this. I felt like I was being called a liar, but, as I told her, 'the numbers were all eights and nines'.

She went on through the sequence of events, encouraging more detail than I had thought to give Claire when she took the statement. More and more images came flooding back to me, including one of Jessica standing in the bathroom with a red rash on her abdomen, which I described as the size of a plate.

When the Coroner had finished, she offered Philip Havers the chance to question me. He immediately picked up on the temperature readings, asking me if my memory now was better than when I had made the statement. I was flustered. I didn't know what he was getting at, or how to answer, but logic dictated – of course it would have been better eighteen months ago.

The Coroner interrupted him, questioning my statement's validity because the copy exhibited and included in everybody's bundle was unsigned and undated. I felt trapped, as though I was about to be hauled over the coals for a simple mistake. But Philip Havers had the answer: 'Perhaps I can deal with the matter in this way, your honour.' Then, with his help, I affirmed the time and accuracy of my statement, which, because I was under oath, was accepted. We moved on, to my relief.

'What size of plate was the red mark on your wife's abdomen, Mr Palmer?' Philip asked me. Again, I was taken by surprise as I hadn't ever thought about it. I had to go right back in my mind and see her, hear her voice, remember our conversation, before answering: 'About an eight-inch diameter plate.'

I wanted all this to end, for the nightmare to go away. My memories were far stronger and more vivid than I wanted them to be in a public court, and I was struggling with my composure. Also, I was well aware that this was my barrister giving me a grilling. What would the others be like?

In the event, when their questions came, they were few. They gave me opportunities to contradict myself, but I had to disappoint them. I felt nothing but contempt towards them. Although a Coroner's Court is not adversarial – meaning that there is no intent to attach blame to an individual or party, only to establish the facts – they were representing the other side. The side that had allowed Jessica to die. It was them and us, and with 'us' reduced, by their clients' efforts, to just 'me' I wasn't best pleased at their attempts to discredit me.

When the Coroner released me from giving evidence I had been on the stand for something like an hour and a half and was shattered. I felt the whiteness of my face as I stood up and stumbled across the floor back to my seat, red-eyed and shaking, guided – thankfully – by the Coroner's Officer. I collapsed into my chair next to Claire, relieved that the ordeal was over.

In my left pocket, my hand was clasped tightly around my little bit of Jessica.

Afterwards Robert told me that the solicitor in particular (acting for the hospitals) had been terrified of me.

'Of me?' I asked him. 'How?'

'Because you gave a good, strong and credible impression in the witness box, because the room's emotions were on your side so he didn't want to be seen to attack you, and because he knew the evidence was overwhelmingly going to back up your version of events.'

The day progressed with a stream of witnesses, some of whose evidence was frustrating, others' boring, and some that left me downright incredulous. There were legal questions and medical opinions that the best of us struggled to keep up with.

The Senior House Officer who discharged Jessica was a surprise though. As she gave evidence I could not see any sign that she saw what she had done wrong, or what she had failed to do. Looking at the copy of her notes during our case conference back in June, it had appeared to all of us – Claire, Philip and all our medical experts – that she had not recorded any new temperature or blood pressure observations, but had merely rewritten them from earlier in the day. Now, on the stand, she was initially evasive about the extent of her examination of Jessica, preferring to cite what she would 'normally do'.

Even the Coroner seemed to become annoyed at her answers and asked her to expand on what she would 'normally' do. She then described a full-body examination in detail. When asked why there was no documentation of any examination of Jessica in her notes, she could only explain it by saying she had been distracted by chatting to the nursing staff on the ward. Her demeanour was one of aloofness and arrogance, and I remembered that Jessica had told me she had only talked to the doctor, without being examined.

Next up was Karen O'Connor, the community midwife. Her arrival on the stand caused a hush, and a rustle among the press. Their numbers had swelled and they had been shown to the jury box next to me by the Coroner's Officer.

She gave a differing account of the telephone conversations on Saturday, 26 June 2004 from mine, but one which was consistent with her statement that I had already read. Her claim was that I had told her not to bother coming. When he questioned her, Philip Havers had a surprise up his sleeve: a copy of her diary from that day had been obtained by the Coroner and clearly showed, in black and white, that on that day she had visited another mother who had delivered a daughter at Kingston hospital, on the same day as Jessica. This mother lived on the opposite side of the street to us, about three doors along. It would have taken her less than a minute to walk from the other house to our front door to visit Jessica and, given that I had raised concerns about Jessica's fever, it seemed odd that she had not done so.

There was even better to come, though. When asked why she hadn't taken Jessica's temperature when she did finally visit the next day, the midwife replied that she had forgotten her thermometer.

Philip Havers looked at her quizzically and asked her whether she had asked to borrow ours. She hadn't and she knew it – there was nothing she could say. He moved on to ask about the red rash on Jessica's abdomen that she and I had been aware of and which she had recorded in her notes, now in front of us. Midwife O'Connor acknowledged that she had indeed been aware of it, but had not known what it was or what it was caused by. She had asked Jessica if she knew what it was, but with neither of them knowing why it was there, it was passed over and forgotten.

Philip Havers asked her whether, with the benefit of hindsight, she thought that the correct procedure in the circumstances would have been for her to refer Jessica to her GP.

When she replied affirmatively, Philip Havers stood in front of me, pondering his next question, playing with the cap of his pen. He asked whether she now thought that she had made a mistake in not taking any further action

Again, the midwife replied affirmatively.

The room was in complete silence, everybody's attention hanging on this answer. Then the Coroner spoke. 'Do you accept that you made a gross mistake?'

'Yes.'

'That is a very brave answer.'

Karen O'Connor was in tears when she finished giving evidence, but I hardly looked at her. It is true, she was well aware of the outcome of her inaction, and she showed remorse, but I was seething inside. Hindsight is all well and good, but Jessica had depended on her, among others, and that had cost her her life. Midwife O'Connor left the court-room immediately together with the quiet lady from the back, and was shown on the news later that day leaving the court building.

Attention to our case had just been stepped up, and the press was buzzing.

When the GP, Dr Williams, took the stand, we were curious. We knew that within the time frame in question she could have referred

Jessica to hospital and saved her life, but we didn't know why she hadn't as only two people had been party to the telephone consultation, and one of them was dead. What transpired from her evidence was that, had she been alerted to Jessica's history over the previous few days – either by the community midwife or in the discharge notes from hospital which had made no mention of the tachycardia or the fact that Jessica had been kept in for ten hours until she was seen by a doctor – she would have acted differently and not just prescribed anti-inflammatory painkillers.

The remaining witness evidence took the rest of the day. The Coroner called a short break sometime after five. Philip, Claire and I went into a huddle. I wanted to know if a verdict would be returned that evening or not. I was worn out and couldn't face coming back the next day. We were certain that, based on the evidence heard, the verdict would be the one we wanted, but Philip didn't want to rush the Coroner into returning it, as it could then be open to a challenge. So when the Coroner came back into the courtroom and said that we would reconvene at ten o'clock in the morning to hear her summing up, he reassured me and said it was for the best.

Shattered and frustrated, I went home to the children and a pair of bottles of wine. I looked in on Harry and Emily in their room. They were already asleep in their beds, so I sat on Harry's bed and looked at them both. 'You've no idea, my darlings,' I whispered so as not to disturb them. 'I can't explain now, but I will one day. I hope you'll think I've done the right thing and to the best of my ability. You deserve so much.' And, when my eyes started to fill, I kissed them both and quietly and went downstairs to pour a drink.

Sitting at the kitchen table, I looked at the photograph of Jessica on top of the radiator cover. It had been taken only a few years earlier at a party my parents had given in their garden. There was

Jessica talking to my mother – it could have been just the other day, the memories were so strong. Then I looked along the shelf to a baby photograph of Emily. How much she had changed. Not only had Jessica missed Emily's milestones – first step, first word, being able to manage a spoon by herself – but I had too. Yes, I was there, encouraging and praising her all the way, but I had been so clouded by grief, pain, exhaustion and hangover, that I hadn't allowed myself to relax and enjoy them to the full, and many of those moments are now forgotten, unrecorded and unphotographed. Jessica would never have let that happen, and I felt I had failed them both.

When we reconvened in the morning, I met Robert and Laura around the corner from the Court where we were soon joined by Christine. We read the morning's papers on a car bonnet. 'Husband in tears as he tells of wife's death after giving birth'; 'Midwife admits "gross mistake".' Looking at the photographs taken of me the day before – by a photographer who had walked backwards ahead of me on my way to find some lunch – I realised I had put on the same tie today. In a flash of self-consciousness and vanity I asked Robert to swap with me.

Claire came out to find us and hugged me. 'Are you all right?' she asked.

'Yes, I'll be fine. I just want it to be over.'

'There are press outside the door,' Claire warned. 'Are you happy walking in? I can ask them to put their cameras down if you'd rather.'

'No, it's OK,' I told her.

We walked in together, past a bank of cameras and flashes, it was hard not to feel even a tiny bit of celebrity status, but I knew why they were there, and I knew why I wanted them to be. I wanted the world to know Jessica's name, how she had died and how needless it had been. I didn't want this to happen to someone else. I also wanted others to taste my months of pain and anguish.

Once in the courtroom, ten o'clock came and went and the Coroner's Officer came and explained to us that she had been delayed as her car had broken down. We waited and waited. Eventually she was announced and we all stood as she entered.

The Coroner sat down, apologising for the delay, saying that she hadn't allowed herself enough time and hadn't finished working on her summing up.

When she began, it started to sound like good news. She referred to the Senior House Officer's evidence, saying, 'I have my doubts as to the fullness of the examination and really the honesty of her account,' and obviously referred to Midwife O'Connor's evidence too and her astonishing admission. It sounded more and more like it was going to go the way I had hoped, until about halfway through when she appeared to contradict what she had already said, even saying that she had 'a conceptual difficulty' in arriving at a verdict of neglect. 'There must be a direct causal link between failure to provide care and a person's death. I do not find that in this case.' I couldn't believe what I was hearing. What was she talking about? When she finally said that she found that Jessica had died of natural causes there was a gasp. I sat, holding my head in my hands. What on earth? I had to have misheard.

When we were instructed to rise as the Coroner left, I sat firmly in my chair, only eventually rising – slowly – out of respect for the Crown that the law represented. Tim, sitting behind me, never rose.

'She was murdered. She was fucking murdered,' Tim said to me again and again when we all convened together with Philip Havers in a small meeting room afterwards. Universally, we were all stunned, shocked, horrified, disbelieving and outraged. Natural causes? My arse.

Nothing made any sort of sense.

Philip told us his thoughts and the options open to me. I had three months in which I was allowed to appeal in the High Court, but if successful that would mean going through a whole new

Inquest, with the possibility of the same outcome at the end of it. I couldn't go through it again, nor drag the rest of our families through it, and we now had so much more strong evidence to take on to our civil claim. I felt we had to focus on that now, and it was obvious that was Claire and Philip's advice – as little as any of us liked it.

The press began clamouring for a statement. Having been allowed ten minutes' privacy to have a cigarette outside, I read a statement to the journalists gathered in the courtroom lobby, before being ushered back downstairs to repeat it to the television cameras:

'My wife lost her life in June of last year, at a time that should have been filled with joy and expectation for her, for me and our children, and for our families. Many lives have been shattered by a tragedy that I believe could and should have been avoided. Childbed fever is not consigned to history, but it ought to be. Although I have little medical knowledge, I now understand that the symptoms are well documented and can be easily recognised. Jessica's parents and I strongly believe that something must come out of this tragedy to help prevent anything like it ever happening again.

'Jessica died many months ago, but her name and her plight should be on the tongue of any expectant parent and in the mind of anyone caring for a pregnant or newly delivered mother. I am determined that no other family should have to live through a tragedy like the one we have suffered.'

I was shaking as I finished. Immediately questions were fired at me, which I answered as best I could, but when asked about Harry and Emily, I shut down. I'd had enough and didn't want them brought into it. 'They're really well, thank you, and totally oblivious to today's proceedings,' I said.

'Have you been protecting them?' the BBC reporter asked me.

'Yes – thank you.' Thank you for your time, it's over now. And thank you for leaving my children alone and understanding when I had said that no, they couldn't film them with me. Harry and Emily didn't need to know about most of this, and I didn't want them upset or worried by it.

I walked away from the cameras and down the road. Claire came with me, and when we stopped I was in tears.

'Shall I get someone for you, Ben? Who can I get?'

'I don't know. I don't want anybody.' I want Jessica, I thought. I don't want anybody else. I just want my wife back.

Claire fetched Mum and the others and then left us, saying that we'd speak very soon. After I had chain-smoked three or four cigarettes, everyone looked to me as to where to go or what to do next.

'The pub,' I said, and headed off. I needed a very large whisky, followed by at least a pint.

That evening I had to put on a different hat for dinner with the mothers from Harry's class at school. It was a pre-Christmas mums' social evening and the children's teachers were invited as well. I got drunk and tearful but there were many hugs and words of support. I was trying to fill Jessica's shoes as best I could for Harry's sake and everyone there knew it.

After the Inquest

By the week after the bitter disappointment of the Inquest verdict, I had recollected my thoughts and confirmed to Claire that I would not be instructing her to challenge the verdict. However, in the light of the evidence gleaned, Claire wrote to the Trusts' solicitor at Capsticks, inviting his clients to admit liability in the civil claim that we would pursue.

The juxtaposition between the Inquest and a potential civil claim has always been one that I have struggled to understand, and found hard to explain. In essence, the two have no bearing on one another; indeed they are both testing different things. An Inquest can only look at the cause of death and whether neglect has played a part, while a civil claim can only look at the possibility of negligence. It's a legal semantic that I have accepted, while not fully understanding. Evidence gathered in an investigation for a civil claim cannot, unless the Coroner decides otherwise, be used in a Coroner's court to prove neglect, but the evidence given under oath at the Inquest can be used in the civil claim. This was where our honey pot was. Contrary to many of my friends' belief, we had come out of the Inquest with a great prize. We were hopeful that liability would be admitted, thus doing away with the need for us to continue building a case and possibly having to have it heard in the High Court.

After about ten days, we heard back from the Trusts' solicitors. Nobody would be available at the NHS Litigation Authority to take a decision on whether or not to admit liability until early January. They requested that we cease further liability investigations (as this would have increased legal costs that they could be liable for) until then. While I tried to take this as a good sign, it was immensely frustrating – I'd got the whiff of vindication in my nostrils and had wanted an early Christmas present for us all.

Early January came and went with no word. Then, towards the end of the month we had a verbal answer. Both hospitals were going to admit liability. Three days later I received a copy of a letter from Capsticks: 'We have now completed our investigations and confirm that we are instructed to admit liability on behalf of Kingston Hospital NHS Trust and St George's Healthcare NHS Trust in respect of the tragic death of Jessica Palmer . . . In the meantime we anticipate that there will be letters of apology.'

I cried silent tears as I read the letter. It was a bittersweet victory, but at least there would be no going to court again to fight. The documentary evidence we had presented them with, together with the witness evidence, was unambiguous and although it had taken an indecent amount of time, at least they had held their hands up in the end. I suppose that I had the midwife's conscience to thank for making her see and admit her mistake at the Inquest, whatever else I felt.

What this 'victory' meant though was another escalation in paperwork. I had to provide Claire with Letters of Administration, birth certificates and goodness knows what else, before she could file the claim in the High Court. As soon as she had, we applied for Judgment which was a court order which would formalise the admission. Then began a whole new phase in the proceedings that I had not expected.

I went, for the first time, to Claire's offices in Holborn, armed with payslips for both Jessica and myself, Jessica's A level certificates and degree, payslips for our nanny and extensive details of baby-sitting and other childcare, details of funeral costs and any number of other expenses that I had incurred over the past eighteen months as a result of Jessica's death. The task that lay ahead was to build a Schedule of Costs for Quantum – literally how much Harry, Emily and I would be claiming in damages.

During our meeting, Claire quizzed me on how our lives had changed in terms of domestic arrangements, and how I had juggled work and childcare. In the course of this discussion, two things came to light: firstly, that I had suffered panic attacks and was severely restricted in where I went because of them; secondly, that I was drinking a very large amount of alcohol.

Claire thought for a moment, then said, 'I'm no medical expert, but it sounds to me like you may have suffered what we call a secondary personal injury. How would you feel about being assessed by a psychiatrist? Go away and think about it if you like. There are both men and women I could arrange for you to see, so think about that as well.'

Although I knew I was struggling with day-to-day life, and had been seeing a counsellor every week for the past fifteen or so months, the idea that this might be termed an injury and one that would require a psychiatrist's assessment seemed strange. It hadn't occurred to me that I might be 'ill' rather than just suffering from the symptoms of bereavement.

I told Claire that I would think about it and let her know by email, which I did within the week. She then set up an appointment with a consultant psychiatrist called Dr Denman. I had chosen to see a woman, because as I told Claire – virtually everyone apart from me

– doctors, midwives, solicitor, Coroner and victim was female – so it kept the pattern going. I also thought I might be more comfortable opening up to a woman.

Claire obtained all my GP's and counselling notes and forwarded them on to Dr Denman, confirming an appointment for early March.

Assessments

In the days after our meeting, Claire prepared a second witness statement for me, addressing matters of quantum, and was in the process of instructing a forensic accountant to assess our costs and my own loss of business income; by now I was barely working, only keeping up a very vague, sporadic and unreliable service for some of my more loyal clients, preferring to hang out at Hurlingham School where I could watch Harry, get a proper lunch, and be surrounded by people who understood and cared. Sometimes I did some work there, often I made the tea in the office, but more than anything the school gave me a purpose to get up in the morning, and somewhere to go instead of moping about at home.

I met with the accountant, Gail, at her offices in north London. It was very difficult for me, driving out of my safety zone in south-west London, and I was anxious when I arrived. She had files of case notes, as well as Jessica's and my accounts, several spreadsheets which she'd prepared and a list of questions. For two hours she grilled me about our work histories and how the household finances before and after Jessica's death added up.

For the first time since the whole process had begun I felt it was the two of us – Jessica and me – under scrutiny. This didn't seem fair. To date, the investigation had centred on Jessica's medical management, each stage being a discovery and a step towards justice for her. Now the focus had shifted and I felt watched. It was almost like an emotional rape. I dreaded what the other side was going to do to us.

The following day I had my appointment with Dr Denman. I drove to her house in Chelsea and, having arrived early, I parked up and walked around the block, smoking several cigarettes to kill time.

Dr Denman welcomed me into the house and led the way up to her consulting rooms on the top floor where we sat down opposite each other, on either side of the fireplace.

'Tell me, Ben,' she began, 'has your solicitor made you aware of why you're here?'

'Yes – to see if I have a secondary psychiatric injury and to assess what treatment I need,' I told her.

'OK,' Dr Denman went on. 'I've read some your medical notes and your account of what happened, but I'd like you to tell me about it in your own words.'

'Where shall I start?'

'Wherever you like.'

I started with Emily's birth and ran through it all day by day, hour by hour. The room around me faded as I spoke and I became immersed in a world of some twenty months earlier, crying as I spoke, never being interrupted. When I finished we sat in silence for a moment before Dr Denman spoke.

'Do you see these events like a photograph in your mind?'

'Yes. No, more like a video that runs over and over.'

'How long do you think you've been speaking for?'

'I have no idea.' Was it half an hour? An hour? I tried to work it out based on how long the appointment had been scheduled for.

'Maybe forty-five minutes?' Time had lost meaning as I re-experienced a week of my life – of Jessica's death.

'We're nearly on time and I think I'm going to need to see you again – in two weeks' time? During that time I'd like you to write about your growing up and your life with Jessica – call it "My Story" – your life now and also how your work has changed. Email it to me before you come back.'

After I left I was worn out and shaking. I lit up immediately, before driving home. Why all this fuss? Why so much attention now? Why couldn't Jessica have been as important then as we were now? Come back, Percy – end my nightmare. Please.

For the next two weeks I drank very heavily; only ever in the evening after the children had gone to bed, but it had a bad effect on me throughout the day. I was withdrawn, irritable and very, very tired. I struggled with my homework for Dr Denman, but finally managed to write a few pages, and emailed them to her a few days before we met again:

'My Story'

I was born in St Thomas' General Lying-In Hospital on 20 July 1970. We lived in a Georgian terraced house in Clapham. My mother chose not to work,[1] and my father worked (and still does, for the same company) as a Management Consultant. My parents also had a weekend cottage in Blackmoor, Hampshire where we spent many weekends year round and much of the holidays, particularly summer. My brother, Robert, was born in November 1972, Laura in April 1976 and Charles in October 1978.

I went to school at Dulwich College Preparatory School, through kindergarten and up until I was nine. I moved to a day prep' school in Hampshire when I was nine, living with my aunt and uncle during the

---

1. Mum didn't go out to work, instead opting to work 24/7 as a mother.

week for the first term until my parents sold the London house and moved to Hampshire. They bought a new house and renovated it, which took a couple of years. In the meantime we also moved out of the cottage and 'borrowed' different houses for a while until we could finally move into the new house, albeit with builders also in residence. From about the age of eleven I started to board, still at the same prep' school.

My childhood was interspersed with sometimes extended periods when my mother was ill with, among other things, ME and heart problems. She normally had a 'mother's help' helping to look after us.

I sat Common Entrance at twelve, trying for Eton. Not quite reaching the entry standard, I was allowed to re-sit the following term for Lent entry to Eton. With extra tuition and in a calmer environment, I passed easily and started at Eton in January 1983. Scraping through internal school exams, I nevertheless passed eleven O levels at 'C' grade or higher.

Starting the A level syllabus (Maths, Physics and Economics) the work proved harder and harder and my application lapsed. I also had more and more run-ins with my parents, and was often caught smoking both at home and school. I swapped physics for the less demanding social biology, but never really settled into this and played up to my teacher. Becoming less and less applied to school work, being in trouble more and more and struggling to get on with my parents, I 'referred' myself to the school's psychiatrist.

After consultations and blood tests I was diagnosed with clinical depression. A spell out of class but still remaining at school, a course of amitryptiline, regular counselling sessions and the dropping of social biology meant that I stayed on at school, ironed out some of the problems and completed my A levels, though only passing General Studies (at B grade, taken by everyone with only a small amount of preparation) but not Maths or Economics.

After leaving school, I was accepted into The City & Guilds of London Art School for a one-year foundation course. Living with an aunt and then other family, I settled into London life, eventually moving into a house-share in Waterloo with a cousin and some of his friends after the course ended.

I did a series of temporary jobs for about six months and then set off on my own on a gap year. I went to India, Nepal and Thailand for a couple of months and then went to Australia. After a couple of weeks in Perth I got a bus to Sydney and after finding work settled into local life. Never managing to save enough money to travel further, I stayed in Sydney for about nine months and flew home in mid-February 1990.

After a couple of days at home I went back to Waterloo and started working for a friend of a friend, helping to make sandwiches and selling them for lunchtime around shops and offices. After a while I also started doing some decorating for my aunt and uncle in their new flat as well. Then someone else wanted some decorating and some small jobs done and, eventually, a full-time business was spawned. The size and complexity of the work grew and grew and I got busier.

I met Jessica in February 1993 in a pub in Fulham and we hit it off immediately. It was, though, largely a physical and seemingly superficial relationship and after six weeks I ended it. Three weeks or so later I saw my mistake and told her so. We started again with a more sensible approach, and never looked back.

In the following summer – 1994 – I bought a two-bed flat in Fulham; Jessica took over my rented flat around the corner for six months or so, before she effectively moved in with me, just spending Sunday nights at her mother's house for a while, so that it wasn't a full-time arrangement. (For mother's benefit.) This eventually became a permanent arrangement, and we bought a dog in 1995.

Around 1996, I started doing a small amount of computer work for the company Jessica worked for, but this again grew and grew, and I eventually stopped building work and concentrated on IT work.

In February 1999 I proposed to Jessica and, after a short and rare moment of speechlessness, she accepted. We were married in St Margaret's, Westminster that July. We extended the flat and finished the renovations to it that had been ongoing, before she conceived and ultimately gave birth to Harry in June 2001.

Just before Harry's first birthday, we sold my flat and moved from Fulham to a house in Southfields. It needed a huge amount of work but we felt it was our dream house. We fitted in, made friends with neighbours and worked hard at getting the house the way we wanted it. We sent Harry to a local nursery when he was two and a half and we both worked from home, during hours that suited us.

In early 2003 we decided to try for a second baby, but much to Jessica's (in particular) dismay it wasn't until September/October that she became pregnant. We were ecstatic. We increased our efforts with the house, putting in a new bathroom and renovating Harry's bedroom for both children. Jessica planned meticulously, though she had a much harder pregnancy with morning sickness and tiredness than with Harry. Because it was so different we were secretly thinking and hoping we would have a girl, but would have been just as happy with a boy.

As with Harry, baby was late, but not by as much. On the morning of 24 June Jessica complained of period-like pains, but refused to believe she might be in labour until midday. Within two hours she was in hospital and the contractions were well under way. It was a much, much quicker and simpler delivery than Harry's. Jessica was, being quite small, immensely proud to have delivered an even larger (9lb 13oz as to Harry's 9lb 4oz) baby with no intervention. For a short while we were both ecstatic.

'Life Since'

I was thrown into a whirlpool after Jessica's death. Once the funeral dust settled I felt lost. I managed to organise (rather a friend did) a nanny, which was a lifeline. I could barely look after myself and eat and sleep at the right times, and she kept the children in a routine and looked after them. Emily slept in my room, and Harry was often in bed beside me and we muddled through our routine.

My memory totally went – even when not drinking in the evening I would forget anything and everything. If someone left a message I forgot to listen to it. If I did listen, I forgot to call back. If I spoke to them, I forgot what we had said. When I went out I panicked – in the supermarket, in the High Street. I did start drinking at night after about a month, which worsened my memory. I couldn't go to bed at night, sitting up at the kitchen table until one or two in the morning, but always fell asleep as soon as my head hit the pillow. If I sat on a sofa during the day, I would fall asleep almost immediately. I fed Emily through the nights, and woke when Harry cried or was unwell.

The only work I did was from September, for the Hurlingham School. It gave me something to think about, but most it got me out of the house – I hated being around when the nanny was there, and I hated it when the house was empty. Equally, though, I didn't much like going out in the evening and, when I did, I never ventured out of Southfields.

I felt isolated and that nobody understood me. I didn't see many people, and my parents and in-laws upset and angered me. I felt I had lost my future and my past.

At one month, six months and a year since Jessica died I thought I was 'over' it. Each time I then realised I hadn't been at the previous stage. I think I have stopped pretending – at least to myself – now. It has always angered me when people have asked whether I am better now.

Except for immediately after Jessica's death I have, at times, found it hard to cry – even alone in the evenings I have stifled tears. My one exception was in the car. In late 2004 I would drive in dark glasses, listening to music, choosing a CD likely to make me cry and playing it as loud as I could stand.

I shopped hard, buying lots of things I wanted but didn't need, enjoying the retail therapy, but it never lasted.

I tried four times to put Jessica's clothes away, finally putting them in boxes in the loft. I couldn't stand seeing her clothes every day, but hated not to have them there. In the end practicality gave way – I didn't have enough room for the clothes I was buying.

I have always been playing catch-up with domestic tasks, but the children have always had most of what they needed, even if I have forgotten to buy food for myself.

'My Job'

I have always been self-employed, and have worked when I had work, and worked on the flat/house when I didn't. If I had work I would often work late at night, early in the morning and at weekends. The number of jobs and clients at any one time has fluctuated, but there has always been enough to keep as busy as I wanted, and someone has always been receptive to a website makeover or update if it was quiet.

After Jessica died most of my clients left me alone, calling me only when it was really important. The others quietly looked elsewhere for help, which didn't bother me. I have at times tried to work, but have been lacking in concentration and have been forgetful in the extreme, needing to be reminded again and again and to be chased. Paperwork and admin' have been virtually non-existent and Customs & Excise are permanently chasing me for overdue VAT returns.

The more that time goes on the less understanding some clients have been, and I continue to lose them. Their needs aren't as important to me as the children's and mine, and I don't have enough energy or enthusiasm to go around. The more they chase, the less I want to do.

When I returned for the second appointment, Dr Denman asked me more about my life now and to describe my thoughts, emotions and day-to-day life, whether I derived pleasure from anything and what my concentration was like. All of my answers were negative.

She then summarised her view. The only good news was that she didn't believe I was suffering from post-traumatic shock syndrome. The bad news was that I had agoraphobia, anhedonia, dysthymia, depression and an alcohol dependence.

'You're struggling in a bad way,' she told me. 'There's no doubt that this is what we would term an abnormal reaction to bereavement. You may have a predisposition to this, but that is neither here nor there. Particularly given the amount of time, this is serious

– effectively you have been at a very heightened level of a great many negative emotions. You must be exhausted.'

I wanted to cry. I felt like a failure. 'But it's normal,' I said.

'No it isn't, Ben. This is not normal.'

'But it is for me.' I had got so used to the way I was that I no longer thought of it as a problem or unusual. Therein lay Dr Denman's concern.

Claire had also instructed a care expert who visited us at home. She went through our daily routine – again, before and after Jessica's death – and took notes on every aspect of childcare arrangements: who was responsible for what, who was at school when and how I planned to continue the childcare plans through Harry and Emily's childhood. I felt she was on my side and that she was supportive and understanding of my need to do the absolute best I could for the children, but when Claire sent a copy of the report to me some weeks later, my heart sank. While it complied with guidance notes and government advice, the amount of childcare the expert was allowing for fell far short of what I knew I would need, and the rates were based on national figures, not current local London prices.

I felt let down, not by our expert, but by a system that goes by an outdated book and does not acknowledge the true costs involved. When our claim was complete we would be applying for the top end that we could, and settlement would only be a lower figure. What part of it was going to be cut? The hours of care that I could buy for the children, or the rate at which it was charged, meaning a poorer quality of care? I was hardly working and earned next to nothing, but I envisaged a normal working life again, one day. Would I be able to do this, or would I have to become a stay-at-home dad, only managing meagre part-time hours, no longer able to afford to pay a nanny? Was I capable of being that dedicated a parent? Would I become more and more exhausted and ground down? And what would happen to us?

Letter to Harry and Emily, 2

Sunday 2 July 2006

My darlings Harry and Emily,

It is two days after the second anniversary of Mummy's death and we are sitting around the kitchen table at home. It is a very hot afternoon and both of you are drinking juice cartons through a straw and doing the most beautiful drawings of sharks, shipwrecks and underwater scenes, all at the same time as watching LazyTown on television.

My heart is breaking for you both, and for Mummy who might seem to no longer be a part of our lives. She is. Both of you look and behave so like her it makes my heart weep. She would be so proud of you both, quietly watching you behaving so well and getting on with each other so amazingly.

I know that you both miss Mummy, even more than you both realise right now, and I am trying so hard to fill the void, but it's not possible, and

I am often too short tempered. Never, ever, confuse that with lack of love. You both are my world and I treasure you both. If you would only let me I would hold you tight to me and never let go. I do get angry sometimes, but it is never with you – just that Mummy wasn't allowed to stay with us. You must know that she wanted to, because she never, ever, would have chosen to leave any of us.

Daddy has some more very difficult days coming up, because I need to fight on your behalf in the Court. I wish I wasn't doing it sometimes, but I have to do it for you – you deserve no less, and Mummy would have done so and would want me to do it as well. One day you will understand and know what I have done for you both, and I hope you will be glad that I did – that will make it all worth it, but right now it is breaking my heart that I have to.

The three of us have come through the darkest of days, and yes, there will be more to come, but we are surviving and we will continue to survive. We have to; it's what Mummy would want us to do. However hard it seems, things will be all right again one day, and we can and will always love Mummy for everything she gave us: life, love and the confidence to be ourselves. She would be so proud to see such loving, beautiful and intelligent children.

Mummy and I will love you both for ever.

Daddy

Counter-schedule

In the first week of September I had an appointment to meet with the defendant's expert psychiatrist. I was terrified. I felt like I would be walking into the lions' den. I navigated south London with the help of an A to Z, then looked for somewhere to park. I drove round and round, trying to find a meter, getting more and more lost and agitated. What if I was late? What if I never made it? What would that do to the case? Eventually, I left the car in a multi-storey car park, then set out to find to the right address. Left? Right? Did I come this way? I was hopelessly lost until, purely by luck, I found myself in the right road. Then I walked for five minutes in the wrong direction before realising the numbers were going the wrong way and turned around.

By the time I walked into the psychiatrist's office I was sweating and very uncomfortable. Unlike when I visited our own expert, no effort was made here to help me feel comfortable or relaxed. The psychiatrist was a large, bearded, bear-like man, and the look I got when I asked for a tissue to wipe my brow made me think twice about asking for a glass of water.

'I've read various documents including your witness statements, a psychiatric report and your medical and counselling notes. I've also read your account, which is written in chapter form. Are you planning to write a book?'

'I just wanted to record my experiences for my children when they're grown up. It seemed easier to write it as though it was a book.' How was this relevant to my state of mind?

'OK, I'd like you to tell me again what happened.'

'I was afraid you'd ask that. I really didn't want to.' It felt so intrusive. How dare he sit there and ask me to share my inner thoughts and observations about the death of my wife at the hands of his instructing solicitor's clients? But he insisted, in a way that I thought was cold and blunt.

I wasn't happy sitting here, but I was focused. I was doing this for Harry and Emily as much as for myself. Pursuing a secondary claim for psychiatric illness had, at times, felt unnecessary and greedy, but the amount of damages in this would not have amounted to much in comparison with the main claim, and I wasn't doing any of it for the money, anyway. I wanted it on record that this whole sorry affair hadn't ended with Jessica's death. It continued day after day, and my children were suffering because they had no mother and their father was struggling to meet their needs. I wasn't about to let the NHS wash its hands of us that easily. They had to be aware of the ripple effect that kept on spreading through our lives because of their negligence.

Rather than try and understand me as our expert had, the psychiatrist looked for chinks in my story. The other side would never have said I was in a worse state than our own expert had found, they would only have said it either wasn't as bad as we claimed or that there was no secondary injury. His attack on my story didn't stop at psychiatry though – he had a list of specific questions, I guessed handed to him by the NHS' solicitor – he was their only avenue through which to ask me questions.

My relief when he finally let me go after two hours was enormous. Polite as I left the room, I then swore as soon as I got into the lift and slammed my fist into the wall. Bastards.

When the counter-schedule was served on us, four days late, in October I went home to wait for the postman. What I read then made me lose all faith in humanity. The hours that they listed for childcare – for the time that Jessica would have spent looking after the children – was offensive. Obscene. What mother only spends six hours on a Saturday or Sunday looking after, caring for, cooking and cleaning for her baby or toddler? Rage coursed through me. How dare they suggest that Jessica would have been so bad a mother? Their conclusion was not based on a personal evaluation of Jessica though, but on the 'generic baseline' for 'normal' parenting input, whatever that means. Jesus – if any parent was this neglectful surely they'd have social services banging on the door? The rates they were quoting for childcare as well were ludicrous – you couldn't get a sixteen-year-old to babysit for six pounds an hour in London, let alone employ a qualified and experienced nanny. What world did these people live in?

The total valuation of their counter-schedule was only just over £400,000. It sounds a lot of money, but isn't – not if you're thinking in terms of eighteen years of childcare and support. I'd already had to spend about a quarter of that figure in care, funeral and other expenses. The rest wouldn't last long. How dare they not face up to their mistake and take full responsibility?

I read their psychiatric report on me, which was as ridiculous as I had thought it might be – what did the fact that I had, at the age of about ten, 'made a fuss' when being asked to cut my own verruca out with a scalpel, have to do with my reaction to witnessing my wife's death? How could he say that my agoraphobia was not restrictive on my life when I had told him that I rarely left Putney and Southfields?

Even when I drove down to Hampshire to stay with my parents I had, at times, used a sat nav for reassurance, until it broke. While the psychiatrist's bottom line was to agree with the diagnosis and treatment advice we had put forward, he somehow managed to conclude that my reaction and symptoms were not caused by my experience in the hospital during the hours leading up to and at the time of Jessica's death. Who, with half a heart, could say that?

The Priory

Since late 2004 I had been seeing a counsellor every week, which had, at times, been helpful. But the combination of drinking between one and two bottles of wine every night, my depression and agoraphobia and, now, the advice of two expert psychiatrists' reports, showed that I really needed a more aggressive form of treatment. 'If you don't,' Dr Denman warned me, 'you could find yourself in very serious trouble.'

One morning, after a coffee in Putney, Sally and I wandered into a paint and wallpaper shop to choose samples for redecorating her baby daughter, Lottie's, bedroom. Direct, as ever, Sally made me focus on why I was drinking so much.

'I don't know,' I told her. 'I just don't know.'

'Why, Ben? Think.' Sally was used to me starting every sentence with 'I don't know' and wanted me now to take a closer look at myself and at what I was doing.

'I don't know,' I repeated. 'So that I can get to sleep. So that I don't keep seeing Jessica die, night after night. Because I just

259

can't cope any more. I love my children dearly, but I hate my life and I just need an escape from it. Drink numbs the pain and lets me forget.'

'But you don't forget, Ben, do you?' Sally reminded me that being drunk also enabled me to cry. I wasn't escaping the past at all, I was reliving it, over and over, until I passed out in bed, on the sofa or at the kitchen table. 'Alcohol is a depressant, Ben. You're not easing the pain, you're contributing to it. You need something, but drink isn't the right thing. Why don't you go to your GP and see if they'll give you some antidepressants for a little while?'

'I'm really reluctant to take antidepressants. I took them in my teens and they made me feel drowsy, sleepy and drugged.'

'A bit like the alcohol then, but not quite as bad for you.' Touché. 'Look at you, Ben.' Sally stopped flicking through the colour chart she was holding, took my clammy hand and faced me. 'You're pale, you're sweating and shaking, you're chain smoking and you're not getting enough sleep. You really need to allow yourself a break. You need it and Harry and Emily need you to have it.'

Damn you, Sal, you're right.

Around mid-September I had registered at a new surgery and had made an appointment to see the nurse for a new-patient check-up. When I'd filled in the forms for Harry, Emily and myself, the receptionist had asked, 'Is it just the three of you?' obviously wondering why Mum wasn't registering as well. I let it go.

At my check-up, however, I was more honest and up front. On the health check form I had written against 'Number of units of alcohol per week' a somewhat conservative figure: 97.

'That's remarkably honest of you,' the nurse commented.

'Yes. I need to make an appointment to talk to a doctor about it. I've also got a psychiatric assessment that I should show them.' She raised an eyebrow, enquiringly. 'My wife died in 2004 after our daughter was born, and I had an assessment as part of a court case. I'm struggling a bit with it all – hence the number of units.'

'Do you mind if I ask how she died?'

'She had puerperal sepsis.'

'What's that?'

I was surprised she didn't know, and gave her another name for it, 'childbed fever'.

Her jaw fell ever so slightly. 'I didn't know that still happened.'

Oh yes. It does.

She weighed, measured and cleared me for diabetes, then took my blood pressure. 'You're a bit hypertensive and, as you already know, you drink too much. Best we make you an appointment now.'

I left a copy of my report for the doctor and was given a card for an appointment the following afternoon.

I knocked on the door and went in. The doctor was young, female and heavily pregnant and greeted me with: 'Well, you're in a bit of a state, aren't you?'

My eyes welled and I looked first to her bump and then to the floor.

'I've read the report – thank you for dropping that off,' she went on. 'What would you like us to do?'

'I think I need a course of treatment as it suggests, so I suppose I need a referral?'

The doctor looked at me for a second, then dropped the bomb-shell. 'I think I should refer you to the Priory in Roehampton. Do you know it?'

Know it? Didn't everybody. There was always some celeb' or other checking in or out. But it was for drug addicts and alcoholics wasn't it? I wasn't an alcoholic, just depressed and agoraphobic. I believed that my heavy drinking was just a symptom of these.

'That seems a bit extreme, doesn't it?' I managed, finally. I was ready to get up and walk away, but she was making sense now that

I listened to her. I had to stop drinking so much or I would never sort any of the other stuff out. She explained that I could go as an out-patient – nobody was going to shut me away, which was my biggest fear because of Harry and Emily. The doctor was firm and stressed the urgency. She would fax a referral and my report to them that afternoon, then they would get in touch direct.

I imagined myself sitting in a group, saying, 'My name is Ben and I am an alcoholic' and shuddered. I knew, though, that this was going to be my best hope for sorting out my life.

On my way in to school in the morning I spoke to Sally on the telephone. 'Well done, Ben. Well done, good for you. That's fantastic.' After a cup of tea and a cigarette by the bins at the back of school I went up to Fiona's office.

'Hi, Fi. Can I have a word? It's sort of business and personal.' I shut her office door and sat down opposite her. 'I've been referred to the Priory,' I told her. 'I think I'm in a bit of a mess, and I just wanted you to know that's where I am, that's what's happening.' I could feel my hands shaking as I spoke.

'Oh, poor Ben. Thank you for telling me. And don't worry, you'll be fine.' As I walked out of her office on the top floor of the school, I felt relieved. Relieved that I was going to be looked after and happy that it was all in the open.

But I was also terrified. What would happen, what would it be like?

The next week I had two assessments at the Priory: one was with a therapist who would decide the type of therapy I would need and who best to put me with; the other was with a consultant psychiatrist, Dr Bijlani, who would oversee my treatment and any medication. Both agreed with my view that yes, I was drinking too much, but that it was a symptom of my real problems – anger, depression and agoraphobia. I was signed up for a course of weekly cognitive behaviour therapy (CBT) sessions and Dr Bijlani prescribed me 15mg mirtazipine tablets, to be taken nightly. She stressed the importance of drastically reducing the amount I drank. 'The mirtazipine acts on the same part of the brain as alcohol and will increase the effects of feeling drunk. You may also be over the limit in the morning, so a word of caution there as well.'

I had one more 'two-bottle' evening, then collected my tablets the following day. From then on I halved the amount I drank, heeding Dr Bijlani's advice and started the medication. Although antidepressants take a few weeks to build up to real effectiveness, the combined effect on me of these two measures was almost instant. I still had a very long way to go, but my anxiety was drastically reduced and I felt positive about the treatment. I couldn't see *how* they would do it, but I was sure that they would help me.

When I started my Wednesday afternoon sessions with a therapist, Simon, I was angry, frightened and depressed. 'With good reason,' he told me. 'Who wouldn't be?' His was a different approach from that taken in the legal assessments; this was a sympathetic, Ben-orientated approach.

Slowly, persistently, Simon showed me how my view of what had happened was 'awfulising' – in my head the awfulness of what had happened was off the scale, 200 per cent bad or more. This, as I could see, was not possible. It could only be 100 per cent bad.

'Think of something worse that could happen,' Simon encouraged me one week.

I already could. 'If one of the children was hurt or killed, that would be worse.' This new scenario could only be 100 per cent bad, at most, explained Simon, which meant that Jessica's death had to slide back down the awfulness scale. He was helping me to put everything back into perspective, but I hated it. Although the logic of what he was encouraging me to think and believe made sense, it still was that bad. It wasn't fair, for me or for Jessica.

'Life isn't fair,' Simon insisted. 'Show me where you signed a "Contract on Life" that guarantees a fair policy.' It was simple enough, and I couldn't argue, but I didn't want to believe it. I just wanted Jessica to be alive.

'You're making a demand that cannot be met, Ben,' Simon told me.

My insistence that 'she shouldn't have died' was, in therapy terms, a demand. Her death could not be reversed, so for as long as I was making that demand my mind was locked into a vicious circle. The only way out was a downward spiral of anger and, when that couldn't be resolved, depression. I could only break the cycle by saying, 'Jessica did die, and I don't like it. I strongly dislike it. But it happened.' I had to accept that she was dead.

We covered the same ground week after week, each time from a slightly different angle, as Simon wore down my 'demands', gently encouraging me to change my beliefs about what happened. 'A, B, C,' Simon taught me: 'Action, Belief, Consequence.' The action was Jessica's death and the consequences were anger, depression and agoraphobia. But consequences are caused not by the action itself, but by your beliefs about it. Only by changing my beliefs could I break the chain and lose the consequences.

It was a long, slow and painful process. By the new year, I'd had twelve sessions with Simon. CBT, I was told, is most effective in courses of between eight and twenty sessions. Any more and it can become counterproductive. We were making good progress, but it was slow. So, for one of my homework tasks Simon asked me to take stock and reassess my goal for therapy. I knew what I still wanted, and wrote it down quickly that evening:

January 2007, homework – 'Goal'
I've been asked to write down what my goal for therapy is. Happiness, I would say. Simon tells me that's an unrealistic Utopia. Maybe it is, but what it means to me is to be happy more of the time than I am unhappy.

I'd like to be happy to wake up in the morning and go to work, and be happy to come home in the evening, relishing the thought of putting Harry and Emily to bed, after playing games with them calmly, reading them a story and coping with bedtime naughtiness. I'd like not to fear and dread the running about and high jinks that blight my evenings. To be able to go upstairs in a clear frame of mind and settle them quietly, without reading them the riot act. To know that they are safe.

I'd like to look forward to the weekends, when I have sole charge for two full days without the luxury and support of a nanny. To be able to do exciting, adventurous things with them. Even just to go to a park and feed the ducks, without anxiety and worrying about what time I have to start cooking lunch, and what lunch will be, or whether they'll fall into the pond.

I'd like to be able to relax, and take each moment in my stride, as it comes. I'd like my head not to hurt with the pressure of stress and anxiety. I'd like to look to the future and see hope and make plans, rather than to see fear and the unknown.

I want my children to look up to me and say they're the happiest they could be. They could say this, as they barely know how happy they could have been. I do know, and I'd like it not to matter so much – for it not be like a constant, searing pain in my heart.

In the meantime, the legal case was rearing its head again and was weighing heavily on my mind. Simon could see that it was an issue, and we spent time talking about it. 'All I can do is help you to prepare yourself for it,' he said. 'What do you hope to get from its resolution?'

'Change,' I told him. 'I want that silver lining to the cloud.'

I knew that whatever happened, it wasn't going to make life better for us, but what I wanted was for no other family to go through what we had gone – and were still going – through.

'How can you achieve that in court?' Simon asked me.

'I can't. All I can do is hit them for as much money as I can and hope that it hurts enough to make them change.'

'How much is enough money?'

No figure could ever replace a life. How would you even began to value one? I knew it wasn't even worth trying to look at it in this way, and with our claim valued in the nine-hundred thousands, there was only one figure that I could think of. 'A million,' I answered. 'I want a million quid out of them, but that won't be enough, so I want a million and one pounds.'

'Will it make the NHS change?'

'I doubt it. They have a budget for this. The NHS Litigation Authority has one job: to pay compensation for their mistakes as determined by the courts.'

It had always felt like calculated risk. If you are able to increase your budget then death and injury remain acceptable to the system. The NHS needn't worry about it. Nobody need worry. Just pay off the Palmers, like everyone else. How cheap human life was. If only the money were spent on preventing stupid mistakes, we would never have been here.

'What if you don't get your million and one? How much is acceptable, how small a sum will you accept without it making you angry?'

'There's no answer. I'm already angry and no figure is going to change that. And I know that it's going to be less, much less, not more than we're claiming for.'

'Who are you angry with? Whose fault is this?'

Blame. It would be easy to find targets for my blame, and I have. People that Jessica and I trusted; people whose eyes we looked into and who let Jessica down – let us all down. Their mistakes took a wife and mother from her family, but did that make me angry with them?

'Individuals made mistakes, but whose fault was it that they were overstretched? Who says, "This is enough midwives and doctors"? I'm not angry with individuals. I'm angry with a faceless, anonymous bureaucracy that isn't getting the job done. Who's ultimately responsible? It has to be the Health Secretary. But, is there any point being angry with a minister? There's F-all chance of getting to speak my mind to them.'

'There's no focus to your anger; that must only make it harder.'

What really made me angry was not the individual points of Jessica's case, but the system that doesn't acknowledge that women are dying from childbed fever. It's not a new disease – it's as old as the hills – but nobody seems able or willing to say, 'It still happens. We need to try harder.' There is blanket denial of its existence, and it has, does and will cost lives. Mothers' lives, just at the point when they are most needed and least expendable, when they have a young family to love, care for and nurture.

The money wasn't going to change any of that, but maybe I could – even just a little bit. If only I could find a way.

Settlement

Claire arranged a conference the morning before the settlement negotiation.

'How are you, Ben? How did you get here?' Chris Johnson, my barrister asked.

I laughed. It was a barely veiled attempt at assessing the level of my agoraphobia again. Then, 'In another taxi,' I answered.

I'd had to get there, and through choice I would have driven myself, but with the congestion charge and lack of parking, opted for the same cab company that I had always used for conferences and meetings.

We sat around a table in the basement, together with our experts and surrounded by piles of white lever-arch files, to weigh up each item of our own schedule and the other side's counter-schedule. We picked through both, analysing where our strong arguments were and where we thought we might be vulnerable.

Suddenly, I sensed that we were playing a legal game rather than simply trying to ensure that the actual cost to my family was covered. I hated it. But was I surprised? Not any more. I was sitting with people who were passionate about their work and about standing up for Harry and Emily, but who understood the system. It all came down to what a judge would decide based on the file in front of him, should we end up in the High Court, which would not necessarily reflect the true cost of four hours babysitting here or there, the true age that children no longer require help getting ready for school in the morning or the true hours that a mother would have spent with her children at the weekend and in school holidays. My million-and-one-pound wish was about to be blasted out of the water and my personal claim for injury looked tenuous. Not because my condition didn't exist, but because secondary injury is so hard to prove in court. I didn't mind about this too much – I wasn't fighting for money for myself – but what I did care most fervently about was doing the absolute best I could for Harry and Emily. Nothing could even come close to compensating them, but their new life was an expensive one if I was going to give them half the quality of life that they would have had, and I didn't see why I or anybody else in my family should foot the bill.

What we had to come up with was a figure that we felt was the margin of what we would settle for, and below which we would fight all the way to court. With a reduction to allow for the risk of going to court with the psychiatric claim, £607,430 was that magic number.

I felt sick.

When the conference was over I fled back to school in a taxi, then drove to the Priory for my two o'clock appointment with Simon. I had thought I would take my anger with me into the session, but during the course of the two journeys I had already worked out what he would say to me, and was listening to reason. By the time I sat down opposite him I was resigned, albeit cynical about the law.

I arrived for the settlement negotiation in my taxi twenty minutes early the following afternoon, as Claire had suggested, and sat in the waiting area at Chris' chambers with a book and my iPod in my rucksack. There was no longer any need for the heavy files I had been lugging backwards and forwards; the analysis was complete now and this afternoon would largely be a waiting game – for me anyway.

Wearing the same suit as always, scrunchie and photograph in my pockets, I was anxious and tense. Who was the man sitting in the corner? Was he the other barrister? Logically, he couldn't have been – he wouldn't have been sitting there, waiting like that, plus he would have had the Trusts' solicitor with him. Still, I felt watched and vulnerable. I was relieved when Claire arrived after a few minutes with her wheeled suitcase of papers and files and her assistant. When Chris came down to meet us, we went out into the street, along to the next-door building and took the familiar lift upstairs. This time we went to a different conference room, with oak panelling, a large dining-like table and a tray of tea, coffee and biscuits on the side. This was where I would spend the afternoon and early evening, with my iPod and Claire's assistant for company. The other side would be on another floor and Claire and Chris would shuttle between the two rooms, negotiating, advising and asking for my instructions. This was going to be a multi-room poker game. But what sort of a hand was going to be dealt to me?

Chris went to meet the other side and show them to their room. When he came back they were in tow. 'They'd just like to meet you and say hello, Ben.' How convivial. How charming of them. Their solicitor had met me before – he had cross-examined me on the stand – but the barrister didn't know me from Adam. Was he testing me? Checking out the opposition? He marched into the room and straight round to my side of the table.

'Good afternoon, Mr Palmer. I'm the barrister acting for the Trusts and we're going to try and get you some money.'

How kind. How generous. How patronising. He extended his hand to shake mine and I took it. Bugger. Damn my parents for teaching me manners, I thought as I shook his hand. It had been spontaneous and without thought, but I hated myself. I didn't want to make peace. Not like this. Not now.

They left us again, and our team settled down around the table, files open, and poured teas and coffees. Our schedule of damages claimed for £986,584.90 and their counter-schedule amounted to £407,222.92. We had set our low limit, but had to decide whether to start the process with a figure lower than our claim, or wait for their first offer.

For three hours we played the game. We went to the seven hundreds, they refuted my claim for psychiatric injury and went to the high four hundreds. Claire and Chris went back and forth. During one of their absences my iPod froze, leaving me with just my book to read – a John Grisham legal thriller.

We reiterated some of the strengths of our case and they went to the low five hundreds. I had, by now, given up all hope of any semblance of justice and just went along for the ride. But was I selling out? Was I standing firm enough for Harry and Emily? Did it even matter? I could have drawn a line and said, 'See you in court,' but how unfavourably would a judge have reacted, and could I take any more waiting, stress and anxiety? I thought not.

We reached an impasse at £575,000 and £650,000 respectively. For a while it looked as though we wouldn't reach settlement – it was almost six o'clock and I feared a repeat of the Inquest where we were called back the next day.

After another round of negotiations, Claire followed Chris back into the room, clutching her papers.

'We think they've reached the upper limit of their authority at 575,' Chris explained, 'but they've asked, if they can make a telephone call – assuming there's an answer at this hour – and manage to get authority for 600, whether we will settle?'

I shut my eyes and thought. I hadn't wanted it to go so low, but I wanted an end even more. 'Let's just do it,' I told him.

'OK. We'll make it a one-time offer, valid only tonight.'

I sat with my head in my hands, eyes closed. A while later they came back into the room. I looked up.

'Congratulations! We've settled. We've just got to agree the wording of the court order and then it's done,' Chris told me.

'Thank you. Both.' My eyes welled and I sat back, slumped in my chair, while he went to write the terms of the settlement. I was shattered, but relieved, and was glad when I heard that the other side had slipped out quietly.

'I've got my car outside, Ben – can I give you a lift home?' Claire asked, as we stood downstairs by the clerks' desks where Chris was looking up on the Internet how to un-jam an iPod for me.

'Yes please, are you sure?' Claire knew me, my emotions and my anxieties so well by now, and she also knew how this stage was for her clients. Home, for me, was only a little bit out of her way, but this was a great kindness, meaning I wouldn't have to sit in a cab with only my thoughts for company.

'I had a word with them before they left,' Claire told me in the car, on the way to Southfields. 'I pointed out that the Letters of Apology were a classic example of how not to apologise. I suggested that they have another look at them, so I hope you'll get a proper apology.'

'Thank you. It won't be the same – having to force it out of them – but at least I'll have something better to show the children one day, if they do rewrite them.'

Little things like this, throughout the whole process, were what made Claire such a brilliant person to have as our solicitor. She was always finding ways of making it just that tiny bit more bearable.

This conversation was also, it transpired, the start of goodbye. Claire told me she was leaving to go to another firm in a month or so. She would be able to see me through the settlement approval hearing in court, which would most probably be at the time we had booked for trial as a fallback. But she would be gone before the costs in the case were settled.

'Stay in touch, though, Ben. I like hearing from my clients, keeping up to date and knowing how they're doing.'

At my request, Claire dropped me on the corner outside my local newsagent. 'I need to buy some wine,' I told her.

'Just the one bottle I hope?' Claire smiled at me.

'Just the one. I'd get far too much grief at the Priory otherwise.'

When I got home I was tired and I ached. I went up to see Harry and Emily in their beds and kissed them both.

'It's over, Harry. I love you, my darling. I love you and Emily so much, and it's all over.'

Harry stirred. 'What, Daddy?'

I'd thought he was asleep. 'Just some work Daddy's been doing. It's finished now and I'll tell you all about it when you're grown up. I love you so, so much and so does your mummy.'

Harry smiled and rolled over, clutching Bear close to him. He was fast asleep again.

It really was over and we had won. We had beaten the mighty NHS monolith. But I didn't feel a shred of victory and the only cause for celebration was that we wouldn't have to take the case to court.

Jessica had delivered her beloved daughter on the NHS and she had trusted it. In return she had been chewed up and spat out. We had been forced through a long, drawn-out, painful and degrading process and then handed a sum of money to go away. To the NHS our family was no more than just a closed file and a number in an accountant's ledger.

High Court Approval

With the court order drafted and approved by both sides, and our claim schedule recalculated to a total of £600,000, Claire and I wrote another two press releases in advance of the mid-March High Court settlement approval hearing, one for release the day before and one for immediately afterwards.

'You realise the papers will only focus on the money?' my father had said to me when I told him. Yes, I did, and there was no getting round it. The hearing would again be in public court and I wanted the world to know. I hadn't been able to say anything publicly since the Inquest, and couldn't do until after the hearing. I wanted the world to know that the NHS had admitted liability and paid. We may have lost the argument for neglect, but the negligence case was high and dry. I also wanted the world to know that the money wasn't a Ferrari fund; it had been hard-fought for, to go part of the way towards paying for decent childcare, and as good a quality of life as I could muster for Harry and Emily.

On the morning of the hearing in mid-March, my cab dropped

me outside Claire's office and I walked with her to the High Court. We didn't know how much, if any, press attention there would be – inquests are of far more interest to the newspapers than hearings, where there are no witnesses or breaking stories. Still, Claire asked me whether I wanted to go in through the front or back door of the High Court.

'Front. Definitely,' I told her. This was the culmination of two and a half years' work, done with pain, anguish and no small number of tears, and I was going to walk in – and out – with my head held high, knowing what we had achieved for Jessica and for Harry and Emily.

In the event, the steps were clear, so I relaxed as I went through the security checks and into the cavernous lobby of the Royal Courts of Justice. Claire led the way to the far end, then down the stairs and onto a subterranean corridor, reminiscent of an Underground tunnel between platforms. On either side of the corridor were small courtrooms, each with two doors and a notice of the day's listing on a board between them. Claire led me in and, as she had done before the Inquest, explained the layout. There was the judge's raised bench opposite, with half a dozen rows of benches and desk, built as one unit.

'Chris will sit here, in the second row, because the front row is kept for silks. There's a strict hierarchy in court,' Claire said. 'You and I can sit behind him here, the press sit over there, and their solicitor will sit on the other side, beside Chris. Is anyone coming to support you? They'll be able to sit here behind us, unless you'd like to sit with them?'

I was happiest sitting next to Claire, just as I had at the Inquest, and told her so. Then I told her, 'Christine and my brother, Charlie, said they'd come along. Perhaps I'd better go and find them.' I looked at my watch. We still had five or ten minutes, and I thought I'd better show them the way down.

Waiting for them in the main lobby, I saw Mr Wilson, the Trusts'

solicitor, and moved so that the listings cabinets were between us.
I really didn't want to catch his eye or, worse, have to speak to him.
It was silly – he was only doing a job, and hadn't made it as hard for
me as he might have done over the years. It was what he represented
that I didn't like. The cold, faceless machine that seemed neither to
care nor show any remorse over Jessica's death.

Christine and then Charlie soon appeared through the scanner
and I took them back to the court.

'The lady over there is from the Telegraph, he's from the Press Asso-
ciation, and she's a Court reporter,' Claire whispered in my ear.

'All rise, this court is in session.'

Chris stood and spoke to the judge. 'If it please Your Honour, I
should like to point out that Mrs Palmer's husband is sitting in court,
just behind me. Mrs Palmer's mother is also in court.'

The judge looked up from his file to inspect us.

Then Chris continued, outlining the facts of the case, of Jessica's
death, and explaining how our claim was made up, and that agreement had been reached. He broke the claim down into its different
component figures and said how every amount was apportioned to
each of the three of us. A sum for each of Harry and Emily should,
he suggested, be held by the Court until they reached majority.

'The only question is how the money apportioned to future childcare should be managed. It could also be held by court and applied
for by Mr Palmer, but I submit it would be appropriate to allow
Mr Palmer access to these funds. He has shown good judgment in
providing childcare thus far, and there is every reason to think he
will continue to do so.'

The judge scanned me a second time. I tried to look my most
responsible. 'I concur. Agreed,' he said. Then he summed up, calling
it 'a most tragic case'.

Mr Wilson rose. 'Your Honour, my clients would like to reiterate
how sorry . . .' He was repeating the same thing I had heard before,
that showed neither a hint of humanity nor of sorrow.

Then the judge rose and that was that. Over in 22 minutes.

Outside in the corridor, I spoke to the press:

'My wife died a horrific death six days after giving birth to our daughter. This should not have happened.

'My son cries in my arms at night because he misses his mother, my daughter cries in sympathy and because she never knew her mother.

'I cry for them both, for the loss of their mother – my wife and best friend – and for the joys of motherhood that have been denied Jessica.

'With Mothering Sunday coming up this weekend, I would like the Health Secretary to try explaining to my children why Jessica isn't going to tuck them up in bed tonight.

'Nothing will bring Jessica back or make up for our loss. More than anything I want action taken to ensure that maternity services are improved, that there is a continuity of care so that nothing like this ever happens again and no other family has to go through what we have suffered.'

I thanked Christine for coming, then turned to Chris Johnson, 'I can't believe this is over, thank you so much.'

I was welling up inside and shaking. I didn't know whether to laugh or cry. I was relieved, but it felt a massive anticlimax. The job was done, yet nothing was over – Jessica was still dead and our children were still without their mother. And I still ached for her presence.

Charlie and I walked out of the High Court, over the zebra crossing and straight into the pub. There must be a reason for its close proximity – how many before me had done the same, desperate for a strong drink?

We sat in the otherwise empty pub with malt whiskies and pints and raised our glasses to a fantastic, beautiful and kind mother, wife and sister-in-law.

That afternoon the *Evening Standard* and several papers' websites ran the story: 'Father-of-two awarded £600,000 after wife died following NHS blunders.' The following morning there was more.

There was also specific interest in a longer story from the media. With emails flying between David Standard, Claire and me, we whittled it down to me writing the weekend's Saturday Essay for the *Daily Mail* the day before Mother's Day, and a studio interview with GMTV at 7.40 the next morning.

I went to the TV studios alone. After going to make-up, I sat in the Green Room and went through the running order with a production assistant. The presenters, Kate Garraway and Ben Shephard, would talk to me, ask me about what had happened and resident GP, Dr Hilary, would give medical input. He came to talk to me in the Green Room at one point and expressed his utter shock and horror at the story when he had heard it.

On air, I felt more relaxed than I'd expected. I only stumbled once, forgetting Dr Hilary's name. Leaving the set ten minutes later I apologised to him, but he didn't appear to have noticed. We stood together outside the studio's double sound doors and chatted for ten minutes, at the end of which he said, 'It's been a pleasure to meet you, Ben, and whatever you do, you mustn't blame yourself.'

'I have done in the past, but not any more,' I said, as we shook hands.

He was right: however much I had thought about what I could have done and however much pain and guilt I had forced on myself, the fact remained that Jessica had been in the care of multiple health professionals and they were responsible for her. I wasn't and nor was she. The NHS had made the mistake, and had admitted it.

Now we had to live with the consequences and the what ifs.

Looking Forwards

The night of the approval hearing marked a turning point. Gone were the stress and anxiety, along with the endless reports and statements, revisions and analysis. That evening, Fi, Max, Chris, Sally and I had gone out to dinner. Not a celebration, but a marking of new beginnings for all of us. Sally was starting a Relate training course, Fiona had found a new headmistress for the school and I had a new life to forge, a new goal to pursue.

In our weekly sessions, Simon had prepared me as best he could for the legal case and was now working with me on What Next? He was at pains to point out that for me to continue seeing him week after week at this stage could be counterproductive. Through his perseverance, my depression was lifting and I was no longer the angry man that I had been. The anger was still there, somewhere, but I wasn't holding on to it. I was no longer saying, 'The anger is the only thing that gives me the strength to get up in the morning and fight through each day.' We talked about when we should call our last session. Initially, the thought of not having that hour on a

Wednesday after lunch was terrifying, I had come to rely on it and my week had revolved around it. But on reflection, I realised that it was becoming a chore to drive out to Roehampton and it was starting to get in the way. I didn't need it any more. The consultations with my psychiatrist, every eight weeks or so, would continue for as least as long as I was taking antidepressants, but it was definitely time to stop CBT.

In April, at our last meeting, Simon showed me how far I had come. I hadn't noticed it week on week but he was right. I wasn't 'cured', nor was I 'normal' – whatever that is – but I was in control of my thoughts and emotions, and he had given me the tools to keep working at it each and every day without spiralling back down into my dark hole.

Yes, Jessica was still dead, and no, I didn't like it any more than I did the day she died, but I had begun to accept what couldn't be changed, and was no longer looking so introspectively. What I couldn't accept was what could be changed – the unnecessary deaths of other mothers from childbed fever. Wanting to find a silver lining for our dark cloud had been a 'demand' that worried Simon, but with his help I had turned it into a preference. Granted, it was a very strong preference and a subject that could still make me angry, but it was becoming a much more healthy desire for something – anything – positive to come out of Jessica's death. I knew that she wouldn't have just accepted it, had it been me who had died so needlessly. Jessica would have fought tooth and nail. I had to do something with what I had learned, something that would prevent another family from experiencing the depth of pain and anguish that we had.

Knowing exactly what to do had evaded me for too long. I had been on television and Jessica's story had been reported and written about at length in the papers, but it wasn't enough. Yes, people had been affected by it and had talked about her and about our children in their offices and on the tube as they read the papers. But would that stop it happening again? I had to do more. Yet, the harder I searched for an answer the harder it was to find one.

It wasn't until just before Easter, as we drove down the A3 to stay with my parents, that it hit me: I would start a petition on the 10 Downing Street website. I would take the issue to the heart of government and then I would set up a website to explain what it was about.

I designed the site in my head on the road, and wrote the content over Easter at the kitchen table. 'Jessica's trust' was born. It did tell her story, but most important of all, it gave me the forum to say, 'Look, this is what it is, it hasn't gone away and it still kills mothers – but nobody tells you that.' If I could make mothers, husbands, midwives, whoever aware of how serious and yet also how treatable it is if diagnosed – or even suspected in time – then it just might work.

'Did it hurt when Mummy died, Daddy?' is not your average conversation-opener over tea. But coming, as it did, from a five-year-old boy, it clearly warranted a considered reply.

'The doctors made Mummy as comfortable as they could and, in fact, she was asleep for a long while before she died.' On a ventilator too, but I omitted that bit. 'But, do you know, Harry – the last thing that Mummy and Daddy talked about before she died was you and Emily. She loved you so, so much.'

He beamed. It reminded me (not that I need reminding) why I feel such a strong urge to make a difference. No more children should have to suffer in the way that Harry and Emily have.

Jessica and I knew that life would change when Emily was born, just as it had with Harry's birth, but never in a million years could we have foreseen just how much. Death is always cruel; when it is this untimely it is doubly so. Our world was shattered overnight and we were plunged into the unknown. For a frighteningly long time I could see no way of getting out of the abyss, and day-to-day survival has been harsh and lonely, but with Harry and Emily's little faces looking up at me expectantly, what could I do? Sometimes I have wished that I could have drunk myself into oblivion, but that would have been too easy, and too unfair on the children. I owed it to Jessica and to them to fight on and do the best I could.

The way that I have coped with single parenthood and Jessica's death has not always been popular – at times I have shut us away from the world and from family in a determination to win with a team of three. It is thanks to the family and friends who have allowed me to do this, who have been there on the telephone or who have brought us a hot meal and then left, that this has worked. I don't feel like a single parent though – I'm a double parent, and I will try my hardest to continue to rise to the challenge. Harry, Emily and I are a team as strong as any parent could wish for, and if we have got through this by clinging on to our love for each other and for Mummy, we can take on anything.

Life will never be the same and it will never be normal. We will never forget Jessica, nor will we 'move on' in the way that so many people who haven't lost like we have will imagine, but we can be happy and we can carry our love and memories with us into our new life. I don't know what the future holds for us – we're taking it a day at a time and there will be many more challenges ahead, but Jessica gave us the best grounding for them.

When, for the first time in her little life, Emily came up to me and said, 'Daddy, I want my Mummy,' I realised that she had begun, at the tender age of three, to understand what made her different from her friends and other children. 'Mummy' had been just a concept and a photograph on the bedroom wall to Emily. She had been growing up not knowing what it is to have a mother, just that she was once loved by a beautiful woman.

Harry's pain has been lessening as he adjusts to life without Jessica, and I always feared that Emily had yet to feel her pain. Perhaps she was just starting to now, at almost the exact age that Harry had.

'I know you want Mummy,' I said to Emily as she sat on my knee. 'Harry and Daddy want Mummy too. We all want Mummy, but you know where Mummy is, don't you?'

'Mummy's upstairs,' Emily told me, bright and knowing.

Upstairs in heaven with the angels; Mummy is an angel. Or did Emily just mean the photograph?

I have often talked and thought about 'the tunnel'. It is the period between Jessica's birthday in May and our wedding anniversary in July. In the intervening two months are both Harry's and Emily's birthdays, the time of Jessica's illness and death, the funeral, and my birthday. After that there are no more painful anniversaries until Christmas. In the years since Jessica's death this period has been an emotional roller coaster, but for the first time, three years on, I viewed the end of the tunnel very slightly differently.

I kept myself busy all day, working, but still paused to reflect – as strongly as I'd done the year before – on a markedly different July 24th, eight years earlier, when the sun had shone strongly enough to make it an almost unbearably hot day.

For the first time, I realised that I was happy. Happy that Jessica and I had had that day together, the six and a half years before it, and the almost five years after it. My thoughts about the loss of the years after 30 June 2004 were very different. Although, to quote the bedtime story I was reading to Harry and Emily at the time (Roald Dahl's Fantastic Mr Fox), these thoughts were often filled with 'dirty words that cannot be printed' there is room in our lives to be happy.

Somehow, I am going to make a difference to some other father, son and daughter's lives so that they never know our pain. That will really make me happy.

Letter to Jessica

Darling,

You have no idea how much you are missed and by how many people. Your death has affected so many of us that are left and in so many ways. People have looked at their own lives, and they have made changes – have even given up high-profile careers to be able to spend more time with their children. Your dad has, maybe against the odds, stayed off the drink and has taken up sailing again; he too is rebuilding his life. Losing you has shown us what really matters in life. You know I always felt bad that I didn't have a highly paid career, and the way you told me how we had what was important made sense, but I never really believed it until you were gone. You enabled me to bring the children up and to love them in the way that you would have done.

You were my soulmate and the love of my life. I miss you and I miss your wildly romantic view of the world. I miss you asking me, 'Do you love me, darling?' and then asking some enormous favour, I miss your dark Labrador eyes looking at me through your long hair.

But you've missed so much, Perc. First words and steps, Emily's first tooth and Harry's first lost tooth. Their first days at school and the day they were bridesmaid and page at Laura's wedding.

Emily is so like you, it can hardly be possible. She looks like you in every way and has your personality. How can it be that a child who never knew her mother can have the same determined streak, the same zest for life and the same expressions? How did she learn to look at me with your sparkling eyes and say something outrageously cheeky, knowing that she could get away with it by throwing back her head in laughter?

Last Mother's Day Harry decorated a box and filled it with sweets at school. He wrote on it to you, 'Mummy was a very pretty gell. I loved my Mummy'; and he often writes messages saying, 'I miss my Mummy so so so much.'

When I stand out in our garden, like we used to, I sometimes hear Emily sitting in the bathroom, gently singing a word- and almost tune-perfect rendition of 'Twinkle, Twinkle Little Star'. My heart bleeds for her and for Harry, as well as for what you have lost.

I ask myself, what can I do to make their lives better? I know where my weaknesses as a parent are and I know where my strengths are. I need to work on some things, but I think I'm doing an OK job, and they are, essentially, happy. You've missed the laughter and the tears that they have shed and there hasn't been a day that you wouldn't have been proud of Harry and Emily; they are brave, clever and beautiful children. I get told it's because I'm doing a good job, but it's not true and I don't like hearing it – you always did a better job and the success is down to you. You set us all in good stead, and it is your love and our love for you that keeps us together and striving to go on.

Looking back at those few days that the four of us shared it is obvious how ill and frightened you must have been. I thought you were tired and bad tempered, and I wish I had known then what I do now. If only we had realised that something was wrong and hadn't felt that complaining would have been making a fuss. I wish I could have had just one more conversation with you. What would I have said? Thank you. Thank you for our beautiful children. Thank you for loving me. I love you; the three of us love you.

The bond between Harry, Emily and I is so strong. Emily is my baby — I have tried to mother her in your absence but I can't; I can only be her father. We are close as you would have been with her though, and Harry and I are so close. The pain that we shared while Emily was still a tiny baby has forged an alliance that cannot be broken. You only have to look at them both together to know how much they love each other. They look out for each other and they are each other's best friend. Our family was broken, Percy, but it is mending. There was once a Percy-sized hole in the family, but it is you and our love for you that has held it together. You are the bond between us that has made us strong again, and we can be happy — slowly I have realised that we can still miss you every day and yet enjoy the time that the three of us spend together.

Maybe I'm finally beginning to come to terms with your death — perhaps now I can finally decide what to have carved on a headstone for you. What can I say? Maybe, 'Friday's child is loving and giving'? You were all three.

In the same way that we always knew we had only been lent our children, maybe we were only lent to each other. I just always thought that the loan would be for far longer. You will never be forgotten; your light shines on for all time — not least in the children's faces.

xxx

About Childbed Fever

Childbed Fever, or Puerperal Fever, was common place in seventeenth-century lying-in hospitals for childbirth because of the lack of hygiene and understanding of infection. Epidemics were common because of cross-contamination by doctors, who often came to treat mothers after performing an autopsy, and who examined woman after woman without washing their hands.

By the mid-nineteenth century there was an understanding of the connection between hygiene and health. An Austrian-Hungarian physician, Ignaz Semmelweis, who is known as the 'saviour of mothers', observed a dramatic decrease in mortality when doctors and medical students washed their hands in a solution of chlorinated lime, despite the practice being scorned at the time.

In 1879, Louis Pasteur identified the presence of streptococcus in the blood of mothers with puerperal fever and the discovery of penicillin in 1928 by Alexander Fleming reduced mortality even further.

Throughout the twentieth century there was a recognised need to monitor a mother's temperature regularly for the first few weeks after childbirth, and a fever in a mother would strike fear in the heart of any family doctor.

Mothers would routinely be kept in hospital for a week to ten days after giving birth, and a midwife would visit her at home, often twice a day, for the next ten days.

In 1982–84 there were no recorded deaths from puerperal sepsis in the UK, but the mortality figure has been rising since then.

Even with good hygiene practice, streptococcus is naturally occurring in the community and can strike down even the healthiest of mothers, causing her death if she is not treated quickly enough.

Since his wife's death, Ben Palmer has been campaigning to raise awareness of the condition, as he believes there are too many avoidable deaths and that the lessons of history should not be forgotten.

For more information about Childbed Fever and on-line references, please visit:

www.jessicastrust.org.uk/what-is-childbed-fever

For more information about coping with child bereavement, please visit:

www.winstonswish.org.uk

Acknowledgements

My biggest thanks go to my children, Harry and Emily, for giving me their love and the reason to keep tackling each day, come what may. Also to my and Jessica's family for their support and understanding, in particular: Mummy, Papa, Robert, Katherine, Laura, Jamie, Charlie, Granny, Gar, Min, Tim and Christine.

Thanks to our friends for their ongoing support, particularly: Jessica's NCT group (Andrea, Fiona, Nicky, Nicola, their husbands and children); Sally and Chris Routledge; Fiona and Max Goulden; the staff and parents of Hurlingham School; Sarah Bokaie and everyone at nursery; and Phil and Karen Irons.

Special thanks also to Ali and Carly, without whom I couldn't have managed.

For their hard work and support during our legal case, I'd like to especially thank Claire Fazan, Philip Havers, Chris Johnston and David Standard.

For introducing me to the writer's world, thanks go to Guy and Annabel, and my immense gratitude to Heather and Elly at hhb and to Ed, Davina, Anne and everyone at Virgin Books, for their belief in, and encouragement of, this book.

My particular thanks to Gill Kirk for her enthusiasm for Jessica's Trust, and to everyone who has emailed their friends about the campaign, posted online in a forum, mentioned my website on their own site or blog, and to those who are helping to spread awareness over coffee.

Thank you also to everyone who has written to or emailed me with messages of support and expressed a desire to help make a difference. Together, we will.

Finally, if you and your children have lost like we did, please remember: you are not alone, and you can find hope.